Entrepreneur:
Power, Myths & Magic

*Dynamic Tips to Start, Create, Grow,
and Maintain Phenomenal Small
Business & Personal Success!*

$ $ $

George J. Trovao
Board Chairman for Golden Horizon Mortgage, Inc.

iUniverse, Inc.
New York   Bloomington

Entrepreneur: Power, Myths and Magic
Dynamic Tips to Start, Create, Grow, and Maintain a
Phenomenal Small Business & Personal Success

iUniverse books may be ordered through booksellers or by contacting:

iUniverse
1663 Liberty Drive
Bloomington, IN 47403
www.iuniverse.com
1-800-Authors (1-800-288-4677)

ISBN: 978-0-595-46341-1 (pbk)
ISBN: 978-0-595-70143-8 (cloth)
ISBN: 978-0-595-90636-9 (ebk)

Printed in the United States of America

Contents

Acknowledgments

I have encountered many people and situations in my life's journey that have had a direct impact on who I have become. Here's a few I need to single out:

As I tried to impart values and knowledge to my children, I discovered they were teaching me more then I ever taught them. A special thanks to my four daughters, Robin Sodo, Tammy Wall, Teri Trovao, and Kim Trovao, and my two stepsons, Timothy Mangum and Jeffrey Mangum.

To my idol Murray Morton of Fort Worth, Texas for his inspirational example as a professional Life Insurance man. His great smile and sparkling eyes as he delivered his motivational talks could move mountains!

My thanks to Bill Basich who partnered up to help with leadership in small town community activities as well as his real estate property management. To Don "King" Kayser for his sharp mind, hard work at Capital Planning Centre, and help in my getting my CLU in life insurance. Both taught me greatly.

My eternal thanks to Jim Roberts for his role in providing a workout gym, teaching marketing ideas, and organizing a mastermind motivational group that helped expand my thinking.

John Davis, Stanford & Harvard Law school grad for guiding me on my Real Estate phase with his terrific advice and encouragement. And for always being there.

My sincere appreciation and gratitude to Robert Gager who lifted me up when I was down by becoming my "guru" in the mortgage business. Also to Bill Jones, a farmer and investor backing us up in our new mortgage venture, always with a positive word that we would succeed! (They are both gone but never forgotten.)

To a sincere, warm gentleman, Steve Pesqueira, who was the first to come aboard our mortgage company twenty-five years ago **and is still with us and going strong.** We are forever grateful for his sense of urgency, loyalty, and responsibility, as well as his way of doing it all in a gentle and loving manner.

My thanks to Tom O'Connor, who came aboard at our Sacramento office as a commercial loan officer. He provided the synergy needed in our start-up days and became a good friend and confidant. I take pride in having introduced him to Jeri, now his wife and soul mate.

Two special sisters entered our lives nineteen years ago, Sharon Sunquist and Cheryl Pavelchik. They became loan officers skyrocketing to fame and success as the best in the west. I have such great respect for their hard work, sharp minds, and great sense of loyalty to both their families and our mortgage company. They are very special people!

Tony Wall, my son-in-law, runs the daily operations of our mortgage company. I'm so thankful for the gift he was given to understand, implement, and update all computer systems, as well as his sense of responsibility and evenhandedness with our corporate associates. Even though he's an Englishman, we still think he's a top-notch guy, and we depend on him.

Thanks to two of my corporate associates: First to my personal *consigliore*, Joe Wirsing, for his enthusiasm and advice over the years. Second to Ryan Stoddard, who we appreciate for his sense of urgency yet gentle hand; I thank him, and I know he will go far.

Thanks to my financial advisor, Judith Davidson, PhD. She's very good (and in the style of Henry Ford, I now have my PhD)!

Last but not least, to my guiding light ever since we met in 1968— my life's partner and soul mate, Lana Stockton Mangum Trovao.

Preface
Why read this book?

How would you like to find ways to become a prosperous, successful, well-balanced man or woman **who is** appreciated while avoiding the pitfalls and stumbling blocks that doom others to failure?

George J. Trovao has spent forty-five years trying to find his way, first making it, then losing it, then going through a period of discovery leading to the way lessons learned can create a dynamic combination of actions leading to ultimate *success*.

Yes, your author learned from others, but find out how calling each new step in creating a small business an "experiment" catapulted him to great success with the least amount of effort and pressure.

This book contains fifteen chapters loaded with the good, bad, and ugly of starting your own business and becoming a prosperous entrepreneur in the world's greatest country, the USA. How? By allowing you to understand the downside and assimilating the upside leading you to a lasting and exciting journey of health, wealth, and prosperity beyond your wildest dreams!

The author reveals long-held secrets sometimes lost in the information age. The book opens your eyes to why a universal power exists and how it can be tapped. It also tell you how to come to grips with contemporary ideas such as how a Positive Mental Attitude can trip you up and how to combine twentieth-century working ideas with our exciting twenty-first century hi-tech knowledge boom. Here's a few ideas he will share with you:

$ The "Bloody Pulp" Theory
$ Peanuts Attract Monkeys
$ DY Formula: Duplicating Yourself
$ The Education Myth: True/False

If you are one of millions tired of working for others who has strong feelings about breaking away on your own, but you're not sure how, then you will find a gold mine of nuggets in this book.

Introduction

My name is George J. Trovao, and I'm a first-time author. I'm very excited about producing this book, which is something I've wanted to do for many years. As time has gone by, I've been increasingly enriched by my participation as an entrepreneur in the economic marketplace. Now the timing is perfect to give you a look at my forty-five years of good, bad, and ugly entrepreneurial experience. My ups and downs have turned out great in the long run, and I'm hopeful my history can be conveyed to you in a way you can enjoy. Hopefully by imparting to you the bumps and bruises I've received versus the successes I've obtained over these past exciting years, I can help you eliminate the negative and accelerate the positive.

This book endeavors to delve into three essential areas I call the *power*, *myths*, and *magic*. I expand on each of these and provide you tried and true methods that if properly applied will lead you to a successful, healthy, and well-balanced life. Read carefully and prosper!

• **Power** (chapters 1–7): Part 1 is devoted to giving you the ammunition you need to start and successfully maintain your own business. Are you both suited and prepared to become an entrepreneur? If so, how will you go about doing so? What about finding business opportunities suited to you? Do you know why it's best to leverage into a new business with minimal to zero cash? Or how to recover from shaky starts and retool to success? What's the trick to recovering from a severe setback? How do you use the **DY** (Duplicating Yourself) Formula to soar above your competitors? Do you know the secrets on how to accumulate wealth or why understanding execution by following up and following through are keys to continuous growth and prosperity? Learning, understanding, and applying these ideas and methods provides you with incredible *power*!

• **Myths** (chapters 8–10): Before you plunge into an entrepreneurial pursuit, I need to guide you through a minefield of so-called established truths and explain how you can avoid pitfalls that could lead to disaster. The myths discussed in part 2 will cover such concepts as whether not having a college degree stifles your opportunities for future potential growth—and what you can do about it. It will also indicate why those preaching a Positive Mental Attitude (PMA) at all costs can make you into a pioneer (you know, the guy on the mountain pass with an arrow in his back). These chapters will provide a new look on how to use PMA so it doesn't backfire on you. They will also cover why old truths about taking aggressive action with the fervor of a crusader can make you into a "Bloody Pulp"—and how to avoid it. Other topics include a fresh look at how to keep your best associates and avoid the costs of retraining new people, why keeping your overhead down is a must, and understanding the "Peanuts Attract Monkeys" concept and how it can make or break you. Overall, part 2 shows you how to break through old myths with exciting new ideas that will propel you to the top.

• **Magic** (chapters 11–15): In part 3, you'll learn how what you share multiplies! I will show how this magic comes in the form of real-world results while still opening your mind to a universal concept beyond this little ball we live on called Planet Earth. I also want to show you how the magic of a DY Formula can accelerate you to unknown heights of success while you embark on a healthy and prosperous life journey.

Forgive my bubbling excitement as I take you into a world of self-discovery resulting from my forty-five years of experiencing the good, bad, and ugly of entrepreneuring. But before I begin sharing my secrets, let me tell you a little about the experiences and successes that, in my opinion, make me uniquely and humbly qualified to write this book.

In my early twenties, I spent part of three years at California State University–Chico. I didn't receive a degree and found myself taking a number of dead-end jobs to support four children. At age twenty-nine, scared to death about turning thirty with no future or career opportunities, I was convinced by others that selling life insurance would be my salvation. I didn't believe it, but felt I had no choice. So here's the overall path I've followed to be in a position to give you some valuable and must-do tips as you proceed on your own path:

My first year as a life insurance and financial planner, I was Rookie of the Year for California Western States Life Insurance Company.

Over the next six years I was fortunate enough to be in the company's President's Council, which is the top twenty-five to forty producers in a sales field force of five hundred agents.

At age thirty-seven, I helped form Capital Planning Centre where I honed my skills in estate planning, pension planning, and tax-sheltered variable annuities for teachers. I also grew in my career by attending seminars held in San Francisco by top tax attorneys from New York specializing in forming tax-sheltered limited partnerships, and was ultimately successful in creating and setting up these limited partnerships for a number of new real estate developments.

At age thirty-nine, I created International Property Ventures, Inc. in which I became a general partner of tax-sheltered limited partnerships for senior citizen housing as well as conventional apartment projects. This included strip centers where we set up Laundromats, lounges, and restaurants. However, in 1980 we experienced a "hiccup" in our growth spurt outlined in a later chapter. But we learn from our ups and downs, right? If we can't learn from our mistakes, we're destined for a life in purgatory.

When I was forty-seven, I formed Investors Mortgage Funding, Inc. in Redding, California, a private money lender, home loan, and commercial loan company. Two years later I moved our tiny headquarters to Sacramento, and over a period of years broadened my mortgage brokerage company into a statewide California operation.

At age sixty-five, I created a new mortgage company called Golden Horizon Mortgage, Inc. (GHM) and phased out Investors Mortgage Funding, Inc. GHM was formed as a combination estate and tax planning tool for our family. GHM provides financing for home loans as well commercial loans. Tony Wall, my son-in-law, became the president and chief operating officer for our medium-sized but dynamic company. I currently serve as 'board chairman' and 'officer broker' and happily remain active behind the scenes.

Over the next fifteen chapters, I'll be letting you know everything I've learned. I hope you will find the way I do this interesting and fun, but that this is also hard-hitting information with "teeth." I will be blending personal experiences along with specific truths that I hope will enrich the fabric of your knowledge as you pursue your own entrepreneurial quest.

You will find ideas both new and old in the next few chapters. I promise to expand your thinking and provide some exciting input to redirect and create a new life for you.

Webster's Dictionary defines an entrepreneur as "one who organizes and assumes the risk of a business or enterprise." Although the related term *entrepreneurialism* isn't a word that's used often, it's a powerful one that hits the nail on the head. However, while entrepreneurs have been around since the beginning of time, many Americans feel that the tenacity and willingness to persevere required of an entrepreneur are traits with a distinctly American flavor. Such an entrepreneurial spirit was engendered by the forefathers of this great nation of ours, then perpetuated by their descendants and immigrants arriving from all over the known world. Lucky for us it is alive and thriving to this day!

$ Power $

Part One:

Chapter 1

How can you succeed as an Entrepreneur?

——————— $ ———————

A FREE ENTERPRISE SYSTEM HAS made the United States the greatest, most profitable country with the highest standard of living in the history of the world. Why? It allows for an independent individual to break from the ranks as a worker for life into building a better mousetrap and running his/her own show with the opportunity for great riches and all the good things life has to offer.

Are you cut out to be an entrepreneur?

What's the difference between being a self-starter and playing it safe? What is there in some people that makes them desire more? What does it take to push a person desiring more to take that first—and most important *self-directed* step—to achieve, whatever it might be? Some people seem to be natural followers while others are itching to step out front. The unknown is the scariest thing in the world, but it can also be incredibly exciting as well. Are you happy with your current situation? Would you like the freedom to create your own business? Have you been looking and searching, but fear the unknown? Have you often questioned your boss or superior's decision making? Do you think you could do better? How would you like to reinvent yourself? Are you interested in becoming an independent business person or salesperson with unlimited opportunity to create wealth for yourself and others?

If so, you may be a candidate to be an independent contractor and future entrepreneur. If you desire to start your own enterprise, open your mind to tried and proven eye-opening ideas.

Have you ever heard of the DY Formula?

It's an acronym for "Duplicating Yourself" as a means of accelerating your wealth-building opportunities. But whoa—we're getting ahead of the story. First let's stimulate your thinking as to where you've been, where you are now, and what you may want to do. I hope to help you reach a point where the DY Formula will propel you to greater achievement and an exciting, fulfilled life of untold wealth. Let's continue to set the stage for you!

Can you be your own boss? Or the boss of your own employees?

Consider each of these questions carefully: Do you recognize yourself as a take-charge person in office meetings? Are you the first in and last out each day? How often have you wondered if you could lead a group of people? When your boss sets aside plans you've submitted, and you know implementing them would have helped the company, does it drive you nuts? Do other people respect and appreciate you for your creativity, work, and positive energy? Do you know in your heart that if you had a chance, you could improve your employer's bottom line? If you want to be your own boss, it's essential that you be able to answer each of these questions with a resounding "Yes!"

Leadership qualities may or may not have surfaced for you in the past. **It's possible these qualities have lain dormant and a new focus in your life will unleash a leadership ability you may not have realized you had.** So, don't worry you can grow into a leadership role. Having an ability to work with and direct others is definitely a necessary element for being a leader. However, if your previous employment position has been one of follower, you can acquire these skills by jumping into a new opportunity. Does this sound like sink or swim? Yes! But use your own initiative to contact and learn from CPAs, attorneys, and successful business owners. You can also learn from applicable workshops and books on the subject. You'll soon see you are gaining the knowledge that in turn will give you confidence to make incisive decisions.

A fear of failure is good—it forces us to take the lead! You must dig in your heels. Can you be your own boss and create a successful money-making business? How do you break away from a secure but oppressive situation? Millions of people just like you have wanted to do just that … but how? Read on!

Learn from the Old Bull

Being eager is important. However, timing can be your most critical advantage. When someone becomes overanxious, it reminds me of the story about the Old Bull and the Young Bull. They were on top of a hill relaxing and munching away when the Young Bull spotted a number of heifers coming into their prime grazing in a valley. The Young Bull began snorting and pawing at the turf and excitedly running around. When the Old Bull asked him what was going on, the Young Bull leaped in the air, clicked his heels, and said, "Let's charge down this hill and take on one of those heifers!" Mister Old Bull thought a moment, then suggested, "Hold on—instead how about we amble on down and take them all on?"

However, it's better to err on the side of action rather than procrastination. Timing and planning become your ally, but you must plan carefully. Don't procrastinate, but try to be cautiously aggressive. In the story above, the Old Bull didn't wait to act, but chose to proceed with determination toward his own version of success. His desire to succeed, tempered by his life experience, led him to adopt a strategy that would accomplish his goal promptly, but without his having to move so quickly that he wouldn't have time to plan.

Specific goals create enthusiasm and motivation that become powerful elements in executing and following through on a plan. This is the defining moment on leading versus following. Desire can propel any individual to a position of taking charge. But there can be pitfalls! Why, and what can you do to avoid them? By using a little caution, you may just hit on the perfect opportunity, one that may fit like a glove.

Why is introspection important in determining a leader or follower?

A gut check is necessary to determine if we have what it takes to strike out on our own. It's important to be honest with our deeper feelings. However, we mustn't make the mistake of procrastinating. Procrastinators make the decision to take action *after* opportunities pass them by. They then justify their indecision by thinking they made the right choice by not acting.

Instinct will become a force to deal with when decision time comes. When luck or chance brings you a potential opportunity, and fulfilling your opportunity requires your having some sort of leadership skills, go for it! You can't permit yourself to wait and think about it. Act! If the opportunity requires a firm hand at the till, but you're afraid of the unknown, you must play it out. Probe, attack, and force the issue. Only then back off and see what develops. You may be surprised at the opportunities you uncover and the hidden potential within you! Remember the old saying, *"Luck is when preparation and opportunity meet."*

What do we mean by a pioneer?

On the other hand, there may be a time when being overzealous and highly excited about an opportunity can put you in the position of suffering the fate of a pioneer—a person who while attempting to cross the mountain pass ends up with an arrow in his back! Be cautious but firm. Watch out for those new, exciting opportunities that seem too good to be true, as they usually are. However, it's better to err by acting versus procrastinating. At least if you act and it doesn't work, it may still spin you off to something that may be just the ticket to meet your entrepreneurial goal. Plus you can learn by trial and error—and make it work on your next shot.

How can true leaders fall into the "secure trap" and forever regret it?

How often have you heard the hue and cry of people who have an excellent job with good pay, benefits, and vacation time who nonetheless claim they'd love a change? They say they feel stifled, that the world is passing them by, and that they know there has to be something better for them out there. Yet year after year they continue in the same rut. Why? Security conscious, they are scared to death to take that risk of trying something new and different. It's understandable, but fear of the unknown is a killer when it comes to making a change.

Working in a bureaucratic setting may lull most into a sense of security. However, it is false security if day after day, you're only going through the motions. If you feel the need or desire to move out of the rut, then you must keep your eye open for opportunities. You will never know if you have the skills to take hold, to be a self-starter and leader, until you get yourself into a position to explore your latent, hidden talents. It's never too late!

The library of the present is your computer—use its speed to access Google and other Web engines that can lead you to new opportumities.

A movie you might have seen, *Nine to Five*, showed working gals in a large, wide open space with desk after desk of IBM Selectric typewriters lined up When Selectrics were the peak of office technology, life was good. IBM even came out with a Selectric that had a built-in ribbon for correcting typing errors. Dynamite—it couldn't get better then this! Technology was a godsend.

But what did we know? In just one generation, the high-tech industry and the advent of the computer with all its programs blew the socks off the past. Now not only can we do a thousand things more with the computer at our command than we ever dreamed, but our quest for information has accelerated to a level we never thought possible.

If you use technology, especially the World Wide Web, to check on job opportunities, a "hot button" entrepreneurial idea may pop up that causes your nerves to jingle and your excitement level to soar. This may even be a concept that jumps out at you when you are looking for something completely different. Suddenly and unexpectedly, you have a new idea that matches your **strengths** and desires! You never know until you jump in and get serious. Use the Web engines to check out the red hot industries. You might search for *job trends, entrepreneur job trends, self-employed opportunities,* etc. You can try a variety of these terms in your Web research. Continue to follow up on different headings that may lead you to job paths that push your hot button!

Diamonds in your own backyard!

You will find there are thousands of entrepreneurial opportunities out there. They may be anywhere in the United States, but have you ever read the story of the wealthy Indian rajah who many centuries ago set out to enhance his riches. It goes something like this, as diamonds were his obsession, he spent his fortune on expeditions and digs throughout the world, dying a pauper. Years later, one of the rajah's ancestors razed the rajah's dilapidated home to build a new one on the site. As the workmen dug deep to set up a new foundation, guess what? They discovered one of the world's richest diamond mines. Remember: Opportunities can be right where you're standing.

One of the best-paying job sectors within any industry is sales. Yet most people back off when sales is mentioned as a career. Why? The fear of rejection. When I was in my early twenties, I was invited for the first time to join an insurance sales organization. I said, "No way! I'm not having people slam the door on my foot. Forget it." However, as I approached thirty, I accepted the training and became a field representative for an insurance company, even though a field representative is a salesperson who lives or dies by originating sales.

Of course one of the problems of selling is that you will encounter many 'turn downs'. You become demoralized receiving one 'no' after another until you hear the sweetest sound in the world, a prospective buyer saying 'yes'. Sales people freak out when a prospect says *no*, especially if they have been getting one *no* after another rather than a *yes* (a closed deal). This reaction is magnified when the salesperson has not had enough closing interviews in a week. If a salesperson on a "commission only" contract or on a draw based on a quota doesn't get enough closed deals, there's no income, so living in a world of mostly *no*'s is frightening. It was for me, but luckily I was one of the fortunate people who eventually succeeded. I was taught that each time you get a *no*, you are that much closer to getting a *yes*, meaning if you increase your number of closing interviews, you increase your chances of getting the *yes* sooner.

What did jumping into the sales arena do for me? It opened the doors to the world of financial services. These new doors eventually indirectly put me in a position to form a mortgage brokerage firm at age 47 that later went statewide in California. My experiences in the sales arena and in understanding corporate models on recruiting, training, and motivating salespeople gave me the background to continue and build on my own. I thank the special power out there for giving me the courage to give sales a try.

I'm using my personal story above as an example. Remember: industries are only as successful as their marketing and sales organization. The exciting part is there's top dollars for those who succeed in sales. Who are those people? The 20% of the salespeople who make 80% of the sales and income.

Why does the sales field offer exciting choices?

Our blessed country has hundreds of thousands of bright, able-bodied men and women who may not have received a college degree. Sales offers a fairly even playing field. Why? To be successful, a salesperson needs real-life experience beyond the degree. Real-life experiences in sales are quite different from the theoretical material taught in a college setting. Therefore new college graduates entering the sales field may not have any advantage over nongraduates as both groups experience the grueling difficulties and mental strain required when making those home, office, or business contacts. Trying to close the deal amid stiff competition and living in a world of *no's* may cause many college grad trainees whose degree isn't in sales or marketing to take a second look at the sales field and decide to use their talents elsewhere.

But this is great for the people without degrees! Why? The sales field is very tough. Those without a degree have fewer options than graduates who can more freely choose careers other than sales. Consequently the sales field may provide those without a degree less competition for career opportunities and a greater chance to work their way up the company ladder.

A degree is great, but even more important is having the initiative and experience in a given field—in other words, working up through the ranks and demonstrating positive results by closing deals. That is the bottom line that counts for any aggressive company. Remember that you can hone your skills by doing. Companies that provide workshops and seminars offer an avenue for motivated people to learn and grow within the company's corporate structure. Employees having the motivation and desire to work their way up a corporate structure may also have what it takes to eventually make it on their own as a successful entrepreneur.

Why are the financial fields of real estate loans, real estate sales, insurance sales, and financial planning still wide open?

As successful salespeople don't have to have college degrees, here's where a bright, energetic person without a degree or the opportunities a degree affords can still get in on the ground floor of a sales organization. I know from personal experience that salespeople in the fields above can quite often earn several times more money than their company president. Here are the attributes that are a must to succeed in sales:

- **You must be *aggressive*.** Top salespeople can be extremely successful by being aggressive along with patient, kind, and understanding. Sounds like an oxymoron, doesn't it? Yet persistence is the key to the aggressiveness that ultimately brings success.

- **You must be a *closer!*** A salesperson must be able to get the signature on the dotted line, finalize the paperwork, and make sure the service or product is delivered and paid for.

- **You must have *a sense of urgency*.** Top income sales earners have a unique sense of purpose. They must have a killer instinct upon the sale's close to receive their bonus or commission check immediately. It's absolutely imperative to zero in on each step of the sales process from initial contact to close by pounding away on follow up and follow through. You must have the urgency to close the sale and make sure you get your payday!

The people who have the qualities described above are the 20% producing 80% of the company sales production—and being paid extremely well for it. What does this have to do with being an entrepreneur? If you want to be your own boss and set up your own organization, having a sales and marketing background is extremely important. Step up! Do it! Learning sales and marketing skills along with having a killer instinct to close deals by following up and following through is paramount to running any successful operation.

How can you overcome fear and move into the exciting field of entrepreneurship?

First I expect that you have taken the initiative by coming up with a plan that zeros in on the type of opportunity you may wish to tackle. Make sure you allow for a transition period that gives you a chance to step into the new opportunity without burning your bridges with your current position. What you are doing at this stage is experimenting.

Let's take a moment to consider some definitions for the word *experiment*: "the act of conducting a controlled test or investigation," "the testing of an idea," or "a venture at something new and different." When you call something an experiment, it provides you a psychological bridge. If what you try doesn't work, don't sweat it—it was just an experiment! Also quite often a failed experiment puts you one step closer to a successful one.

Can you safeguard a transition from a 9 to 5 position to entrepreneur?

Be careful not to leave yourself out in the cold if your entrepreneurial pursuit does not work out. One surefire method is to try the new pursuit first on a part-time basis. Once you begin to feel an air of confidence and you start to see the income potential, then and only then should you pull the plug on your current employment. Attempting a full-time leap into a new endeavor should only be attempted when you are spinning off from a known industry in which you have succeeded as an employee and where you have the necessary capital to carry you for six months. Essentially then you are making the transition from a known type of business with the possibility of failure quite remote.

Let's say you have studied carefully and explored all the avenues of a potential business. You've made inquiries into the specific industry. You've invested some money in the purchase and have set aside some capital for the new overhead and expenses. Now jump in full time. You have no choice! You are the president, vice president, secretary, and work force of your new company. *You* are the one expected to make it work! You have to be there full time. Congratulations, you are now a bona fide entrepreneur! You haven't made a dime yet, but you are on your way to riches.

What is the true test of a safe transition to entrepreneur?

Making a move to an entrepreneurial field is more art then science. The best bet is to give the opportunity an honest chance. The true test is: what do you feel in your mind? What do you feel in your heart? Finally, what do you feel in your gut? The gut-level feeling is the strongest when you make that final decision. It's possible this gut-level feeling is tied into that special universal power that we are all tapped into subconsciously. (More on that later.) However, no matter what your gut may be saying, and even though I'm trying to give you positive reasons to check it out and make something happen, I know that fear of the unknown is a powerful force that may dissuade most people from taking the big step.

Be careful not to ride two horses at the same time. Keeping the old position may also be a deterrent as you're trying to make the new pursuit a success. Balance is necessary, but you must keep your eye on what is most important to you over the long haul. When you're not sure, it could be your fear of the unknown—that unidentifiable feeling that keeps you from investing yourself fully in a new venture. I suggest you push yourself by jumping in with both feet, but have a backup plan in case your new pursuit fails. A safety net is **imperative, keep an open door to your prior job, plus having a little in savings to back you up.** Now you can accept your new pursuit as an exciting challenge—one that may change your life and bring greater riches and happiness.

Once you are moving forward as a new entrepreneur, you may encounter a stumbling block or two. Redirect your efforts. It's possible that a quick evaluation of where you are may suggest slight changes that can give you a new life and a more profitable way to go. In the following chapter, I get more specific on how from time to time you must redirect your goals to achieve what you truly want. Remember: if you call your change of plans an experiment, it takes the heat off and allows you to look forward to a redirected positive approach. Let's pursue this and much more in the next chapter, "Rethinking and Retooling for Success."

Chapter 2

Rethinking and Retooling for Success

—————————— $ ——————————

A N ANALOGY MAY HELP to make my point. The old saying, "There's light at the end of the tunnel" may lead you to several conclusions:

1) **Yes, you see the light. Fantastic! You reached your goal!**

2) **Look out! Your light may be a train heading directly at you!**

3) **As you go through your tunnel, you see no light ahead, but suddenly your tunnel makes a turn. Eureka! Lo and behold there's the light!**

However, resist, I repeat, *resist* from feeling down when all attempts at reaching that light do not work. In this and the following chapters, I will be providing a variety of workable plans for you to achieve your goal.

How can you develop a method that works?

In our United States, sales opportunities are unlimited. Whether the product is a hi-tech gadget, a financial service, a type of fuel, or a paper product, every single business needs sales. No matter what business your mind can conceive, you will need to market and sell your product. Breaking into any type of sales force is much simpler then starting your own retail business from scratch. Why? Retail shops or any type of small company need start-up capital—lot's of it. Lenders and investors require specialized experience if you are even going to get a sniff of potential capital for a start-up. Plus, you'll need additional capital as staying power to allow you to keep your doors open until you turn a profit. Salespeople create the backbone of any successful organization. Many corporations will train you from scratch with a monthly draw until you begin to produce or originate sales business.

As organizing a sales business requires expertise and capital as well as a marketplace, I'm suggesting that you don't try it on your own. You will be given specific input later as to how and when you may have opportunities to build for yourself. First you must have learned the craft and have had some initial success. To begin, your best bet is to join a company's sales organization. They pay for your training and tools, they have their own invested capital in product inventory for you, and they provide you a "brick and mortar" place in which to work that's paid by the company, not by you. Why all of this? Whether their products are services or merchandise, companies know their most valuable assets are the salespeople who can sell them.

For those starting out in sales, I suggest working for a company first to get your training. Then if you think you'd like to step into your own start-up business, you will now have gained some power in knowledge and experience of the selling game. An old saying is, "Salespeople are born not made"; this is true, but without firsthand knowledge of your own sales ability, you won't know if you are cut out for it.

But how do you find a company? Use the Web to study trends within our domestic economy. You can visit a company's Web page and get information directly about applying for employment opportunities on their sales team. Don't forget old established industries as well. Some suggestions are established firms selling a variety of services such as insurance, mortgage, real estate, or title companies.

What kind of game plan must you put into effect?

You have now selected one or two industries that tickle your imagination. Your choices should also build a fire in you, create a burning desire and excitement, plus indecision. Indecision is good. Why? Your creative juices are flowing, with confusion and chaos forcing you to take a step up to determine a plan that can take you to your desired goal: building an income and nest egg for yourself and family. Focus is now essential. Once you have zeroed in on a few companies that tap your hot button, get as much information as possible before starting your inquiry and application process. At that point, begin a campaign to submit resumes followed by phone calls to your selected companies within that industry.

Your best bet is to check newspapers and Web sites for the thousands of companies in a particular industry looking for salespeople. If you are bound to a geographical area, make sure the opportunity is where you'd like to live and work. Remember two things: first, preparing resumes is an art form, but fortunately there is abundant literature on this subject. Second, I'm still pushing your thinking into the arena of sales within the industry you choose. Why sales? Your capital requirements are much less than starting a business from scratch. A new business requires not only start-up capital, but you will have a loss of income for six months or more. In contrast, a transition into a sales position means you may have at most three months of reduced income as you'll be joining a firm that will probably pay you a draw while you're being trained. In this case you must cover the difference in what you have been earning and what you may receive during your training. When you start doing direct sales in the field, you will begin to see an improvement in your overall income.

If instead you decide to pick a business opportunity to sell products versus services, you will need capital to cover your own basic needs for at least six months. This is on top of the capital needed to purchase the business and inventory and cover your business overhead costs for six months, including support staff. **When selling products you have the extra costs of stocking your business with inventory and cost of store employees to handle customers. In a sales operation you merely need an office and eliminate the extra burden of inventory**

costs. Consequently, I will primarily direct you toward a start-up career in sales in a service industry and provide you with a path to parlay your experience in direct sales to eventually having your own operation with people working for you and with you.

When is the best time to take action?

It's imperative that you stay with your present position while exploring your options. Continue to put your name in front of every company that is looking for someone like you. This process can be nerve-racking, and you may begin to have doubts about making the leap into the unknown. But doubts can be set aside if you plan from a position of strength. Stay with your present employment while looking for your new opportunity. There will always be doubts and fear of the unknown, but we'll touch on this more as we go.

Why is it a "no no" to attack conventional thinking?

Pioneering can be dangerous. Don't allow yourself to get intoxicated from the ideas of what a company claims to provide. Be especially watchful for the elaborate advertising by companies claiming to offer riches. These companies are usually pushing a pyramid concept, which even if legal, projects a grandiose picture of how within a few short months you can run your own operation. You will be in charge of dozens of people at different levels below you. It can work; however, these companies build their sales from the hundreds of people who have come and gone through their pyramid mill. There are other ways to build as will be discussed in later chapters.

How can you check out and build on the success pattern of others?

Legitimate companies abound in the thousands. As you zero in on one that hits your hot button, make sure you find and speak with people within the organization. Review with them what they experienced versus what was offered. Get their feelings about the way the organization interacts with its new salespeople. Will you have an opportunity there for personal growth? Will the company allow you to fly as high and wide as your aptitude, desire, work ethic, and motivation will take you?

Why are enlightened methods critical to your success and well-being?

Deepak Chopra, an American citizen born into an East Indian philosophy who combines Eastern wisdom and cutting-edge Western science, wrote the book *The Seven Spiritual Laws of Success.*[1] This is a must read! Chopra's Seven Laws articulate how developing a spiritual awareness and learning to listen to our unconscious selves can help all of us achieve our goals and realize our life's potential. Mr. Chopra provides a great reading experience with in-depth teachings that takes us beyond conventional everyday thinking. He opens our minds to the outer realm of consciousness where real power lies. As you might guess, I find his teachings very influential, and I'll continue to reference them in later chapters.

Why may PMA and game plans not work?

What is PMA? It's an acronym for "Positive Mental Attitude," a favorite expression coined in the 1960s that was the end all to anyone wishing to accomplish his or her goals. However, later chapters will touch on how using PMA can backfire. In fact, tying a specific game plan with exclusive use of PMA can create hell on earth unless you're prepared to be flexible regarding the end result of your plan. You understand the story regarding the light at the end of the tunnel? Remember—light may appear where you least expect it.

Why can extremism in any redirection effort be self-defeating?

I've always heard the line from Frank Sinatra's "My Way" not in terms of regrets, but expectations. In my version it's, "Expectations, I've had a few, the results too few to remember". You must have high expectations to achieve goals according to your deepest desires. However, be careful your goals and expectations aren't so tightly

---

[1] *Deepak Chopra, The Seven Spiritual Laws of Success: A Guide to the Fulfillment of Your Dreams (San Rafael: New World Library, 1994).*

wound **up** that they cause you to fall into the trap of falling short and falling apart. Your intricate internal motivation creates a powerful force within to achieve that which you wish externally. Your confidence in yourself can take an immediate nosedive if you put all your eggs in one basket in expecting what you desire to come to perfect fruition. Later we will be discussing protection against such events.

Why may written goals not work?

There may be a dichotomy in what I express to you next. Specific sets of goals are necessary as you develop a game plan to retool for a breakout into a new entrepreneurial opportunity. You must lay out every aspect of obtaining your goal **in writing** to insure your achievement is worthy of your desires. Improbable targets may be the catch. It's very possible that you will be diverted in every attempt to reach the specific goal. With each attempt to secure your goal, you may be met with a variety of setbacks.

At some point you may feel your light at the end of the tunnel is a train coming straight toward you! Do not give up, never give up! Each negative that you encounter is telling you something. Detour! Take that bend in your road. Get a reading on it, and continue on the redirected path. There may be many turns in the road to securing your goal. Take each turn as a lesson and maneuver by repositioning your direction to a new path. The path of least resistance may be your ticket. However, your desire is an absolute must to keep your confidence up at every turn. Consequently even written goals may have to be constantly revised to get you to the promised land.

Why do people neglect their planning for success in work and life?

Average Americans spend more time planning their annual vacations than their own future. It is a *must* that you sit down the first of each new year and set out what it is you'd like to accomplish that year. Then every quarter at the very minimum, you need to review your goals, study them, and make any additions or changes.

Understand goal setting is an art, although some writers feel it can also be a science (more on that later).

Short and long-term goals must be written out in a simple, easy-to-read, and understandable way. Your short-term goals are what you see happening in the next three months, six months, or year. You also need to spell out where you want to be in five years or in the next ten years. Don't relegate your goals to just your business, job, or career. Your goals must provide a balance in your life for you to be truly happy and prosperous.

What are the seven safe harbors for daily living?

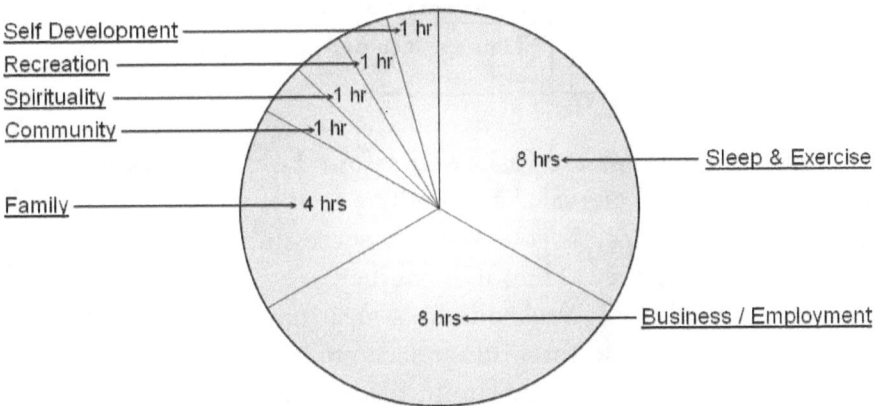

Remember, maintaining a balanced and successful life depends on how many hours a day you choose to spend in each "safe harbor." **Example, If you spend to much time at work you may be cutting down on valuable time spent with family or if you spent to much time in recreational interests you could be reducing the time needed to be successful in your job or business , causing financial hardships.** What may be important to you may have no relevance to someone else! However, where you spend the most time will have a definite impact on who you are and who you will become. How do you take stock of how you spend an average day? The following seven safe harbors can give you valuable insight as to how you spend your average twenty-four hours:

THE SEVEN HARBORS

FAMILY	Time spent with spouse and children
BUSINESS	Time spent on job, career, or business
HEALTH	Time spent on sleep and exercise leading to a healthy body and mind
SELF-DEVELOPMENT	Time spent on personal improvement
RECREATION	Time spent on play, relaxation, and mental healing
COMMUNITY	Time spent "giving back"—involvement in social and civic affairs
SPIRITUAL	Time spent in prayer, affirmations, or meditation

Remember: there are just twenty-four hours in a day. If you spend more time in one safe harbor of life, it takes you away from your other harbors. Balance is your key to a successful daily work routine and planning for a rewarding life's journey. Also: you do have make-up time on weekends! Weekends are a great opportunity to use your sixteen hours set aside for work and commute time to catch up on your other harbors, especially family, recreation, and spiritual.

Will you ever have enough money to feel completely secure?

Money alone is never enough. People who obsess about how much money they can accumulate may find what they seek, but the pay a price in terms of reducing their time spent in their other six safe harbors of life. Even once they have a million dollars, they'll still be insecure, feeling they need two million; when they get two million, they will want three. It's never enough. Why? The feeling of never having enough seems to be a human trait, a driving force caused by the need for absolute security. But money can't replace people who love you unconditionally or who make you feel wanted and needed. When you share love, you get love. When you share your knowledge and desires, you get back love and desire. When you give back to your community, it gives back to you. When you share in your creation of wealth, wealth comes back to you.

What is the universal power, and how can it help you with your daily living and achieving of your grandest goals?

A special universal energy does exist. You may call it by the name of any god or religion of your choice. Even if you don't believe in any of these, just the belief in existence will do. A powerful intelligence does exist throughout our immense universe. It manifests itself in the power and energy that comes into us and emits from our own bodies and minds, including our subconscious! Sages throughout time have written volumes about the connection between the conscious and subconscious minds and a special energy religions call spirit. As you read along, you will become aware of some of the methods you can use to attract and utilize this greatest power in the universe!

How can you tap into universal power through affirmations?

Your mind channels the power of the universe. Humanity has tapped this universal power since the beginning of time. Some call it prayer or meditation, both of which are a form of affirmation. Affirmations are desires, wishes, goals, or remedies for our concerns; they can be written and reviewed or memorized and silently expressed. When you write your affirmations as goals and review or silently express them twice each day, you create a powerful magic in your life.

What is amazing is that as you express your affirmations, you will find yourself attracted to the very things you wish to have happen. Plus what you wish will be attracted to you! Over thousands of years, philosophers and writers have advised us that our subconscious mind is always awake. Consequently, expressing your affirmations consciously allows the subconscious mind to work for you and direct you consciously. (More on this later.)

How can using mentors redirect your actions to success?

There must be someone in your life you feel has been an inspiration to you. By making contact with successful mentors, you can copy some of the successful strategies they used to achieve their own goals. Don't be afraid of approaching a potential mentor, Why? They are proud of their accomplishments and will be happy to share with you. Take what they have to offer and do it your way by putting your own imprint on it and moving forward.

How do relationships provide the anchor for success? It is imperative to your breakout as a successful entrepreneur to ally yourself with like-minded and like-thinking associates. Why? They provide the positive energy you need as you move through the tough times of getting started in a new enterprise. Like-minded associates may also show you how to reach your four steps that require some expertise as you get a business under way:

- Your first step was having an idea for a new breakout business or career.

- Your second step is making a commitment to start your new career or business.

- Your third step is having the expertise and/or capital to open up a business or make a career move.

- Your fourth step is operating a successful moneymaking operation.

More on this in later chapters. But let's face it: besides developing solid ideas and creating a terrific game plan with all the due diligence you can muster up, you must associate with good, responsive, and highly motivated people. The human element can't be overemphasized. Your ability to draw to you these quality like-minded associates is one of the most important ingredients for your success. In later chapters, I will be discussing a "sharing of the wealth" concept as it relates to your associates. This concept will also be your bedrock to a phenomenal future of growth and riches.

People in business or sales careers often become confused as to who is their competition. A constant refrain may be, "There are just too many people or businesses in the same field, and this competition is killing me!" Let's examine the concept that looking into your mirror is what you get. If you give your mirror a negative look, guess what you get—a negative response. But give the mirror a positive look and guess what's reflected—a positive response. Life is a 100% reflection of your actions. Every single thing you do from your first look into your mirror in the morning to the last look in the evening is who you are! The only true competition you have in your business or sales life is *you*.

In the beginning, you make your habits, but in the end your habits make you. Nothing in life is truer than this. How can you guarantee that *you*, not your competition, controls your destiny? Just follow these crucial *success steps*:

! **Set up next week's meetings this week.**

! **Carefully plan today your daily activities for tomorrow.**

! **Use yesterday's planning as a "heads up" to start each new day.**

! **Follow through on meetings with motivation and zeal.**

! **Use a killer instinct to follow up and close prospective deals.**

! ***Do not* wait till tomorrow to complete calls and paperwork—*do it now*!**

Remember: the habits of those you consider your competition will also allow them to rise or fall based on their ability to follow the above steps to success. Their habits will make or break them as well. However, taking the above steps will melt away your concerns about competition. As you begin to see your income grow, an amazing event will occur: your motivation will multiply! Why? A wave of enthusiasm spreads throughout every fiber in you body. The above steps will instinctively become part of every moment of your thinking. Success is no mystery when you're following your new game plan. **You will discover you've become a truly successful and happy entrepreneur** by following these success steps to the "T."

Chapter 3
When the Earth Stood Still
$ ————— $ —————

BEFORE GOING ANY FURTHER I believe it's important for you to know that successful people may have many 'ups and downs' in there business career. It's often expressed that before success there's failure. The question then is how can you come back from failure? Let me open a door in my life allowing you to relive through me one of my real down times!

What is the day that for me will last in infamy?

You may think it was December 7, 1941, when the Japanese Imperial Navy launched a surprise attack on Pearl Harbor and hurled the United States into a horrible global conflict. But *no*—it was *not that day.*

For me, it was October 6, 1979, a day that will last in infamy for my lifetime. Paul **Volcker**, the Federal Reserve Chairman, was making a historical decision to "break the back of stagflation." *Stagflation* was a new word that had been coined to define the appalling and fatal path the U.S. economy was on in the last days of the 1970s. We were experiencing runaway real estate value appreciation up to 15% annually combined with interest rates over 10% that created an intolerable inflationary spiraling effect. With double-digit interest rates and double-digit inflation in the United States, the dollar was losing its value so rapidly there was a national fear we could fall into the same trap as South American countries with their Third World economies. Consumers would need a wheelbarrow full of currency to buy their groceries. Consequently the Fed had to step in heavy to stem the negative tide and stop stagflation.

What could be done?

Up steps Mr. Federal Reserve Chairman Paul Volcker, all 6' 9" of him, with his answer: raise interest rates until you break the back of inflation! Why were inflation and double-digit interest rates a killer? Inflation reduced the value of how much our dollar could buy, and double-digit interest rates brought borrowing to a halt. High interest rates were a killer to anyone who had borrowed to make purchases or create new ventures. With the blessing of the Reagan administration, Volcker continued to hike interest rates to an historically unprecedented 18.5% prime. What did this mean to commercial and multi-housing real estate as well as housing values? The bottom fell out of market values. When people tried to sell a property, quite often they discovered there was a bigger mortgage than their property was worth, which means the property had a negative value that gave them a net worth of minus zero! It was a bitter pill for U.S. entrepreneurs like myself to swallow, however, we knew it was the only way to save the patient, meaning the U.S. economy, rather than unsuspecting fledgling entrepreneurs like me.

How did using OPM produce exciting results, but set the stage for disaster?

OPM is an acronym for "Other People's Money." The theory was that you should borrow as much as you could and purchase real estate, as with values going up 15% a year, how could you lose? You could also create investment partnerships in which investors put capital into a tax-deductible real estate limited partnership and purchased more real estate (this was called limited partnership syndication). Then you leveraged whatever capital you obtained from both sources to purchase more real estate. This pattern continued as you leveraged yourself into more and more real estate. As real estate values had been on an upswing, this was a sweet way to catapult yourself to great wealth. Minimal cash down payments for wildly appreciating real estate property purchases allowed you to create a ton of equity growth. You could then refinance the new equity growth and turn around and buy more properties. It was fantastic, as there was no way you could lose, right? *Wrong!*

Does this sound familiar to stockholders who borrowed against their NASDAQ stocks and purchased more and more hi-tech securities in the 1990s? This also happened in the building boom in the early 2000s. Low interest rates and zero down payments motivated investors to purchase of single-family homes and condos that were then resold at a phenomenal profit within six months. No way could these investors lose, right? Again wrong—by 2006 the bottom had dropped out of the home sales market. This trend continued into 2008 as home values plummeted leaving the latest investor buyers and home owners holding properties worth less than their mortgages.

Why do income tax loopholes create a financial illusion?

The IRS did its part by closing tax loopholes, which included prior IRS rulings allowing certain opportunities to shelter investments. When the IRS felt shortchanged, it pushed for new rules eliminating those legalized shelters. Our government needed to recover potential lost income and stop the drain on the U.S. treasury caused by the prior IRS rulings. For example, in the 1980s, limited partnerships allowed a **general partner** to bring in ten investors (or up to twenty-five through special IRS exemptions) as limited partners, who were the private investors essentially capitalizing the limited partnership. An attractive incentive for these investors/limited partners was having no liability beyond their initial investment plus receiving a ton of tax deductions they could write off over a five-year period or less. Based on the type of real estate such as a housing development purchased by the limited partnership, investors could at times have a tax write-off of 60% of their investment in the first year!

Thus the investor could save a lot on current taxes owed and yet have a terrific opportunity to obtain capital gains treatment on the profit from a sale within a five-year period. A person like me could create a limited partnership and serve as the general partner both directing the activity of the limited partnership and participating in a percentage of the equity position. Sounds great, right? But what you never know is when the IRS may drop the hammer and put a quick stop to various legal loopholes. Depending on the U.S. economic cycle at a given time, factors can stack up against entrepreneurs leaving us in perpetual purgatory. You the reader are beginning to get an inkling of your author's personal story, but there's more, much more.

How can leasing place you on the brink?

IRS rulings have come and gone along with the so-called investment tax credit (ITC). The ITC was a terrific boon to stimulating the economy by encouraging equipment purchases, then allowing the purchaser to write off 10% of the full purchase amount directly against the tax due the IRS, even if the purchase is financed. This was fantastic! Another exciting tool still existing to this day allows people to lease everything and write off payments for such items as furniture, vehicles, Selectric typewriters, etc. (Can you believe it: in the **1970s there were no computers and in the 1980s there were very few computers?) By leasing everything, you had a direct write off against business net income.** Terrific, right? The benefits of leasing is that you can avoid tying up your capital in equipment purchases. While purchased equipment can be depreciated only over x number of years, 100% of your lease cost can be written off against your taxable income annually. Phenomenal, correct? Or is it? What's missing in this exciting plan to accelerate tax deductions and increase your cash flow? What happens when the Fed and the IRS change the rules about various deductions or dramatically increase interest rates? The opposite effect can and will occur: a drastic drop in your ability to maintain a steady cash flow—and when cash flow disappears, you're dead in the water.

What does it mean to be over mortgaged?

This is an insidious thing that can happen to real estate property owners. It could be owners of single-family homes, condos, apartments, or office and retail buildings. Beware: we are now entering dangerous ground. *Over mortgaged* describes the situation when a real estate owner borrows against his currently owned property to make new real estate investments during a hot market, which is then followed by a cooling market that reduces the sales prices on those properties. If a large correction in property value occurs (i.e., plummeting property values), guess what? The lowered value may be less than the mortgage, meaning more is owed on the property than it is worth. This can be especially nasty if you own a bunch of limited partnership properties completing their fifth year so they are now up for sale. How much equity (difference between the mortgage amount and the current market value) do you have in this property now? Answer: nada, nothing, zip! This happened to many people in the early 1980s, and it happened again in 2007/2008. Unfortunately these lessons were learned too late. I can guarantee whoever this happens to will have this lesson firmly and forever implanted into their subconscious minds. However, if you can learn from my experiences, these lessons can prepare you to avoid potential pitfalls.

How could $10 million in gross assets and $3 million in net assets disappear overnight?

Houdini the great magician could not have pulled off a greater and more effective trick than what the U.S. economy did between 1980 to 1983. Paul Volcker, the then-Federal Reserve czar, orchestrated a perfect coup over stagflation by skyrocketing prime interest rates to an all-time high. In his defense, it needed to be done; a U.S. economy with a dropping dollar could not be tolerated. High interest rates broke the backs of a U.S. economy out of control, and it did it primarily on the backs of highly leveraged real estate investors across the United States as your author can personally attest. Prolonged high interest rates caused property values to precipitously drop. Commercial property values are ruled by net return on invested capital. Higher and higher interest rates drove the net return lower and lower, resulting in properties valued at less than the mortgages taken out on them years earlier. In this situation, what happens to your investment portfolio value? In your author's case, gross assets dropped to $7 million from $10 million, effectively wiping out $3 million in net worth overnight. Dead in the water!

How does one deal with despair?

Cash flow is gone; payments to leasing companies are due; mortgage payments and rental payments are due; credit cards are borrowed to the hilt. Creditors want your blood, your children, your next of kin. On top of everything a threat was made to make due a $50,000 demand note. A private lender claimed your author's financial statement contained false information, and if the underlying debt was not paid in one week, he would go to the authorities. Wow! Even though this claim was untrue, it was a kick in the solar plexus. I had a loving spouse and six children ranging from high school through college depending on me! The pressure, the pressure.

How do you float new money from your bank at 21.5% interest, the highest in our nation's history? How do you request money from investors when their current investments have gone sour? You don't. You are alone on an island of despair. No assets, no cash flow, no hope. When the news hit regarding the $50K note being due in one week or else, I felt sick to my stomach and headed for home mid-afternoon. Staggering to my bedroom I found myself falling to the floor, flat on my tummy as I clubbed the carpet with both fists. I was sobered when I heard a hoarse voice crying out, "Why me? Why *me?*" It was my voice. I was forty-four years old, experiencing the worst financial nightmare of my life. Paying off the $50K demand note wiped out the last of my assets. I was at the bottom of the Grand Canyon with no way out!

Where could I go from here?

First thing to do was establish if I had any credibility left with any of **my investors, lenders or creditors.** I had to take the full blame for my failures. Using a football metaphor, I was a quarterback forcing the play, trying to do too much. Taking on a full load, thinking my gut-level instinct was always right, and aggressively pushing each play my way. Not listening to experts around me when I didn't like their message. It is said, "A football quarterback takes too much of the credit and too much of the blame." This is true. However, knowing this didn't take away the bitter taste of defeat or help me overcome incredible feelings of failure. I had to start from ground zero and blame no one but myself.

When you're feeling low, down and out, you need to reach for emotional support. Where can it come from? In my case, I had a person with unswerving belief in me—my life partner and spouse Lana. My children were devastated for me, and siblings who had provided financial help worried about me and prayed I could somehow pick up the pieces and get my financial life in order, which included paying them back too, of course.

I recall visiting Gettysburg, standing next to the bronze statue of General Lee on a rolling hill, and looking out over his battleground on the third day of battle. I read where he commanded General Picket to make a last big charge against the Yankees and break their battle lines. The author explained how the colonels, majors, captains, lieutenants, sergeants, and soldiers on the firing line were in the midst of bullets, cannon fire, smoke, and hand-to-hand combat. Death and carnage was everywhere. Collectively they had only one thing in mind: *survival!* They couldn't think, plan, or organize, just survive. Whereas General Lee was on this small hill, a spyglass distance away from the fighting where he had time to confer, plan, and organize, I was the half-crazed soldier on the firing line wondering how do I survive *now?* I had to step back, way back to a small hill in my mind, and see if by surveying a lost battlefield, I might learn something from it and survive another day.

Does everyone flee a golden vehicle when it becomes a sinking ship?

Living in a small rural area meant any successes I may have had were overblown and possibly exaggerated. The common hardworking folks and small merchants there struggle to make it work for themselves. A local youngster catapulting forward and riding high may cause considerable controversy. There are those who resent the success of a known and local entrepreneur while others may seek you out. They want a piece of your thinking process—and the synergy that goes along with it. But then when your ship capsizes and you're trying to find a life vest, guess what: those who envied your success are laughing. Bringing someone down to earth from his lofty perch is worthy coffee-klatch conversation. Where are your defenders, your business associates, and your former Investors? Gone! You quickly realize you've been deserted by everyone except your attorney and CPA. What friends did I have left? *None.* However, every cloud does have a silver lining, and mine was a beautiful and giving spouse who believed in me no matter what!

How do you fight on with no weapons?

When we're lower then low, down and out with nowhere to turn, we may go back to some of our earlier teachings. I was brought up as a strict Catholic in a family where Sunday church and Sunday school were mandatory for all the children. However, one may stray from the autocratic teachings of a church. I did by evolving into a more universal concept of the spiritual. (More on this in a later chapter.) However, what I did do was request a key to the local church so I could get in at 7:00 a.m. each morning, light a candle for my beloved mother, kneel, and allow myself to get into a semi-meditative state. I would then recite to myself a number of affirmations.

This gave me the mental and moral strength to face each day and battle the myriad challenges then facing me. I would end my affirmations by singling out one or two specific areas needing immediate attention—the goals current and future I hoped to achieve—then allowing the information to go from my conscious to subconscious mind. I could then walk out and lock the church door with a feeling of calm spreading throughout my being and a special energy I knew would carry me through the day. No weapons? Guess again! What I've suggested above may not be for everyone, but it was powerful medicine that sustained me and allowed me to fight another day.

How do you rise from failure and find hope?

My spouse and I were in our forties during this bleak period. We had a common bond working for us: short jogs with intermittent walking. Jogging was always tough, but having your partner there to talk to and let out all your inner emotions and concerns gave a respite to the drudgery. It also did three things for us. First, it gave us a discipline, a feeling we had control over something. Second, it was a way to maintain physical fitness. Finally, it was a fantastic way to brainstorm and draw strength from one another.

I recall a memorable day when we had jogged about a mile into the countryside just outside of our small community's fairgrounds. As we then started walking and talking, we kept hitting on a recurring theme: "Where do we go from here, and what will we do?" It then struck us, that even though we were flat broke, we were healthy, we looked reasonably good, we had decent mental faculties, and we felt like we were as good as many others who'd done well. We then made a pact: *back-to-back* we could take on the world and fly as high and wide as our energy, health, diligence, and enthusiasm would allow! Somehow we would make it back.

What now? We then began a campaign to create various plans with plausible opportunities. We determined that I could possibly pursue my former sales career in the insurance business or get my real estate broker's license and acquire information to start a mortgage company. Combining this plan with my wife's considerable talents created a synergy that allowed the two of us to become much greater then the sum of our parts. We set out goals regarding geographical areas we'd like to work within. We described various entrepreneurial pursuits we would attempt—pursuits dealing with some of our past experience and know-how. It was tough and it was rough. When you lose all you've worked for, you also lose your self-esteem and confidence. So it was with me.

How do you overcome doubts and re-establish confidence?

Looking back on my later forties, I went through a metamorphosis when looking for potential entrepreneurial positions in the insurance field. It was a real eye-opener to be talking to managers or supervisors in their later twenties and middle thirties. Mostly these were people assigned by ownership or corporate heads to talk to this "over-the-hill guy." "Young Turks strutting their stuff," I called them. Why Young Turks? Because they hadn't experienced the knocks life can give you. They had all the answers as they were flying high, quite full of themselves. I know—I was one once! It takes getting kicked you-know-where a couple of times before you can grow up professionally.

These interviews were partly demeaning as well as embarrassing and awkward. I was being lectured by infants on sales and organizational approaches and how I must "walk a certain line" or else. But what could I say? I had failed in my own endeavors and was broke. So all I could do was say "yes, sir" and "no, sir." My guts were churning. Somehow I needed to get some control.

I tried looking back, then evaluating where I'd been and what I'd accomplished. I then looked forward, deciding on what options I should choose to produce us a cash flow. Finally, I decided not to take on any opportunities with our Young Turks and instead get my real estate broker's license. I still needed to earn again and very soon. So in laying out one goal at a time, striving to find a direction that could work and taking it day by day, I reached a conclusion: I would establish a game plan to start a mortgage company from scratch.

Will I ever make it back?

Goal setting is one of the most powerful tools at our disposal. You write down goals. You read them when you start your day, then read them again before turning in at night. Miracles happen—you are either directed to the very goals you wish for, or those goals magically come to you. Quite often you may reach your goal indirectly. (More on this in later chapters.)

Back to my setting up a mortgage company. This was accomplished through a circuitous route. First I was hired to be a consultant for a corporate mortgage company. The corporate stockholders had no viable funding sources, plus as they had too many irons in the fire, they failed. I then was contacted by others in the area to start my own mortgage company. I did! But starting a new company and hoping it will take hold creates a new, intense pressure. My confidence had been shaken badly from my previous adventures. Worry and anxiety took over, and a fear of failure gripped me.

So how could I use my past experiences to withstand my uncertainty and be able to function while trying to succeed? I decided to take a new tack: anything I tried to accomplish would be considered an *experiment*. Why? Because when you're trying an experiment, there's always the potential that something may not work. Therefore within the idea of an experiment, you are free from putting yourself in concrete. You have flexibility, and if it doesn't quite work out as you planned, you make adjustments—you bend rather than break. An experiment also gives us a psychological out; as you know going in you may have to redirect, reexamine, and redo your complete game plan, you *will not* allow yourself to force the issue and become a "Bloody Pulp" (more about this in later chapters.) Another psychological helper is to lower your expectations. Don't drive yourself crazy. Later as you begin to build your company's income potential, you can adjust and shoot for higher income goals, but don't heap this kind of pressure on yourself going in.

How can there be light at the end of a dark tunnel?

Aha—you may think this is a deep, mysterious secret? It can be explained logically. Generally you would think of a tunnel as being a straight shot from one end to the next. However, consider this: you are proceeding through a tunnel with no light ahead, but then you reach a point where a side tunnel allows you to make a sharp right turn. You make a right-hand turn and enter the side tunnel, but it's still dark. Suddenly the tunnel makes a left-hand turn and *eureka*, there's the light!

This analogy illustrates how when all seems lost, if you persevere, take action, and continue to move toward a specific goal, quite often you will reach the goal not as you intended, but indirectly. You can choose opportunity or stick to your guns, but guess what? Either way, things and people will be directed to you or you to them. And incredibly there is light at the end of the tunnel maze. Keep in mind what has been advised earlier: you must know when to back off and take another run at it. *A great big warning:* There is some irony here, as it sometimes happens the light at a tunnel's end could be a locomotive heading directly toward you. Be *aware*, and *do not* become a Bloody Pulp again! (See Bloody Pulp Theory chp 9)

Using minor techniques as outlined above, I was able to make an exciting comeback in a challenging and profitable entrepreneurial pursuit. It was not exactly as I had first planned, but unexpectedly it was better! It brought to mind a line from Shakespeare's *Julius Caesar*, "There is a tide in the affairs of man that which taken at the flood leads on to fortune." I now understand what he meant. Being able to position yourself and never giving up is essential to placing yourself on a path launching you to success.

What three intuitive actions most influence decision making?

As I proceeded through the metamorphosis of being down and out through the stages of a comeback, it became clear to me three intuitive and instinctive actions were at the center of every decision I made: the heart, the mind, and the gut:

1) **Your heart reacts with emotion; listen to it, but don't let it be your final arbiter.**

2) **Your mind can be both logical and easily excited, but it can be a fairly good judge of your final choices.**

3) **However, in the final analysis it's your gut that may give you an intuitive reaction based on your conscious mind drawing from every fiber in your body and your subconscious. Listen to your gut—it's usually right on.**

How can you accelerate your wealth-building potential? In the next chapter I will explain how I stumbled onto a wealth-building program I refer to as the "DY Formula." In future chapters I'll cover how to tap the power within as well as sharing the wealth techniques that can lead to creating incredible well-being, wealth and prosperity, and happiness.

Chapter 4
The "DY" Formula

——————— $ ———————

How can you "Duplicate Yourself" to create outstanding wealth?

By using and properly executing what I have coined as my "DY Formula," you can propel yourself in any type of sales, marketing, finance, or production organizations to create a continuous string of other people to duplicate your work. It's an exciting way to increase and multiply your own income-producing efforts by either training or proselyting others to expand your production. The concept is that you allow others to duplicate your own efforts whereby they share in the wealth. You create a vehicle allowing others to fly as high and wide as their own motivation and desire may take them! Yet the vehicle you created also allows you to control and channel your people's duplicated efforts in a lucrative manner by working within a system you have set up and coordinated. How and why this is possible will be illustrated as I uncover the inner workings of a simple plan.

When did I discover this method?

I stumbled onto it after years of trying to build a mortgage company. My approach had been to keep costs down and do commercial loan production on my own surrounded by a few top-notch loan originators. However, this merely provided my wife and me with a living. My first clue to potential income growth was a piece of innocuous information I noticed in a pamphlet sent me through the mail. As I began to throw it away, something caught my eye. It was a quote from Napoleon Hill, author of *Think and Grow Rich*; I don't have the words exactly, but I remember it as being something like "It is an eternal truth that people receive more pay for their ability to get others to perform than they could possibly earn by their own efforts."

I continued to read the article, which outlined some interesting points that had an immediate impact on my psyche. I don't remember exactly what it said, but the idea was that when the North Carolina Creative Leadership asked successful business people about what sets great bosses apart as teachers and coaches. I took from it the following ideas:

THE BEST TEACHER/COACHES:

1. **Counsel: They give younger or less-experienced associates constructive advice and feedback. They use younger associates as sounding boards.**

2. **Excel: Whether in marketing, finance, or production, great boss/teachers are the best in some aspect of their business.**

3. **Give exposure: They make sure that the work and accomplishment of young associates gets seen by others. They open doors.**

4. **Provide latitude: They give associates freedom to try and the courage to fail. They involve them in important tasks.**

5. **Challenge: They are tough taskmasters and demand excellence.**

This article opened my eyes to something so simple that we overlook its power. Napoleon Hill's thoughts hit the nail on the head and reawakened my conscious mind to a basic truth: you can earn x amount of money by doing it all yourself; however if you duplicate your own efforts by having good people amplifying your work, you can triple your earnings. I took a look at my own strengths and decided I possessed some of the five traits above, which meant I could as a boss be a good teacher/coach. The next question was: how do I put this method to work?

How can this method be implemented?

First you must have a desire to be your own boss and participate in the American free enterprise system. It's important to have some or all of the five traits listed above along with a burning desire to succeed. In my case it was a desire to rebuild some kind of income-producing operation that could provide for the last two decades of my earning years. In addition, I felt a deep need to prove myself to my spouse and children as it was very important that they be proud of me again. This intense desire drove me to obtain my real estate broker's license and start up a private money lending company.

Through the 1980s, banks and savings and loans handled financing for businesses and home purchases. However, an individual borrower had to have excellent or near-excellent credit to obtain financing. Consequently there was a vacuum created for a mortgage broker to step in with a private investor to loan money to potential property owners who were not able to secure financing through conventional means. For example, through mortgage brokers borrowers with sizable equity in their property but lousy credit could still secure a first or second mortgage on their property and extract a sizeable amount of capital for themselves.

However, private money loans were expensive, as a borrower might have to pay fifteen points upon loan closing plus a much higher interest rate than conventional financing. However, in those days when borrowers couldn't obtain sub-prime financing, the private money broker filled the breach. The broker provided much-needed dollars for the borrower while creating a nice paying investment to the private investor/lender willing to take on a little extra risk when lending their own funds. It was a perfect partner to our private enterprise system as it created a flow of funds circulating throughout the economy. It was good and I loved it!

My original business plan was to create a small mortgage company with at least one knowledgeable associate in a small market area in Redding, a city in Northern California. However, I needed to have a group of private investors willing to lend to what we called a "C" or "D" borrower. (These are borrowers with rough credit and unstable income, but who have excellent equity in their property.) We then advertised in local papers that we had money to lend when banks or savings and loans (S&Ls) said no. This plan worked; however, it failed to create enough cash flow to support two families. A critical decision was made to move to the much larger market in Sacramento while keeping the start-up office in Redding going with my new and later lifetime remarkable, hardworking, sincere, and honest associate Steve Pesqueira.

Thus after we had created our original plan involving Redding, we put it into effect by physically creating a new company. We then began a mission of sorts as to how we could get this private money lending operation started and earn income. Of course the objective was to build a positive organization that in turn would provide my associates and me with an income for ourselves and our families. Consequently we decided a move to Sacramento with its different demographics and larger metropolitan base extending south in California's Central Valley to Modesto was in order while Steve continued our first branch in Redding. Our move helped open up new loan business opportunities in the Sacramento Metro and the Central Valley areas, thereby allowing two families to begin making a decent living.

We adhered to a basic tenet I had come to embrace: "It's an experiment." Calling our new company an experiment gave us a psychological edge. It also gave us the flexibility to constantly adapt to changes rather than adopt only a single course of action. We wanted to avoid becoming a Bloody Pulp. In the late 1980s, a cataclysm occurred in our S&L industry that turned financing of residential property on its head. Scandals rocked the industry regarding the junk bonds being pushed by CEOs who pocketed millions. The S&L industry that had been designed to finance real estate home purchases had collapsed— and it was now gone.

A new breed of companies called mortgage bankers entered the fray. These companies provided wholesale rates to mortgage brokers in contrast to the S&Ls that provided only retail rates. Consequently a mortgage broker couldn't offer a good deal to a potential home owner, and thus previously had been shut out of the residential loan marketplace. But now mortgage bankers needed the mortgage broker with their retail loan agents to sell their loan products. It was a perfect fit. I decided to recruit a couple of people with prior experience in the then-defunct S&L business, specifically people licensed with DRE (California Department of Real Estate) who had hands-on working knowledge. They would know how to network and acquire new loan borrowers, negotiate a fair loan rate and terms, plus process a loan package acceptable to our approved mortgage bankers. Fantastic!

We now expanded into doing "A" residential loans, which are loans to borrowers who have top credit and top income. Soon we were advised to secure Federal Housing Association (FHA) approval with the U.S. Department of Housing and Urban Development (HUD). This opened up a new market for loans that allowed lower-to-middle income borrowers to purchase a home with a minimum down payment. As many mortgage brokers did not have the net worth to become approved with FHA/HUD and we did, it opened up opportunities for my little company to recruit loan agents (originators).

DUPLICATING YOURSELF!

Obviously if we did all the work on loan originating ourselves, we'd get 100% of the commission offered to the mortgager broker by the mortgage banker. It was then I discovered Napoleon Hill's wonderful truth hitting home: "*It's an eternal truth that people receive more for their ability to get others to perform than they could possibly earn by their own efforts.*" I then started a campaign to recruit first-class professional loan originators throughout the state of California, which included setting up regional and branch offices in Southern California. Our company would offer considerably more in commissions to these recruits, essentially giving them an immediate raise in pay! I'm also a firm believer that "what you share will multiply, and what you withhold shall diminish." It's not a religious belief, but more a practical and spiritual belief. I'll get into this more later.

Originators who proved themselves had the opportunity to become full-fledged entrepreneurs by having their own branch office and receiving a 100% commission if they had one or more originators closing loans. In addition, the branch manager would receive override commissions on each of their own branch agents. In this way we could duplicate ourselves many times over. We were not getting the big direct commission we were receiving at first, but the small override commissions we did receive from a larger volume of loan production provided for a wonderfully profitable company. I know this sounds easy; however, I'll be following up with critical input on how it required a synergistic effect that allowed the whole to become greater than the sum of its parts. You have to have a team that clicks together and a driving inner force to achieve, but there's more, much more!

Why do many fail trying?

Let's get back to how our experiments and lessons may be of help to you. People desiring to build for themselves must have a driving force to succeed. Not everyone has it. There has to be this power inside down deep that keeps you motivated. It is something with you when you go to bed and with you when you awaken. Each day you need to take tiny steps towards tweaking your business vehicle to a point it does create income and profit for you and your associates.

Failure can occur when the power in you to succeed begins to sputter. You've encountered too many pitfalls you don't believe you can overcome. You may not have the ability to change gears and try a new tactic or experiment. If there is no way for you to achieve business success and the money to sustain the program you're building runs out, then it's possible you have to back off, call your plan an experiment, and move on to something else (or as is often said, try to get a real job, as entrepreneurship may not be for you). Obviously you can't Duplicate Yourself if your finance, marketing, or production sales organization can't get off the ground.

What are the key ingredients needed for success?

Let's move back into the area of building a successful operation and dealing with myriad ideas detailing what you must expect of yourself to reach the brass ring. Let's assume you have several of the traits listed at the beginning of this chapter. Plus you feel you have untapped potential as well as the desire and motivation to succeed. You now have set up an office and launched your particular business. An important ingredient is to have a well-thought out business plan and begin executing it.

Next and so very important is to *follow up* and *follow through*. Your company and your credibility will be judged by how promptly you follow up and follow through with your clients, customers, and associates. This cannot be emphasized enough as there is no question in my mind this is a make-or-break for most organizations. You must instill in yourself and your associates on how important it is to get back to anyone—a client, vendor, new recruit, bill collector, or disgruntled complainer—and to do it that day, *now*, or at least never more than within twenty-four hours. Why would you delay? A couple of reasons you may not call back ASAP could be you know the caller's concern is being handled so why bother to call, or you may think you're too busy to call back. Or maybe you're waiting to get the info together for your caller before responding in the future. But *no, don't wait!* Your caller is anxious to know something even if the something is that you don't know. A call diffuses your client's anxiety and builds a goodwill bridge for you that is great for public relations. *Follow up now!*

Follow through has to do with telling someone (an associate, client, investor, vendor, new recruit, or especially a disgruntled client) what is intended to be done and when you'll do it. So many start-up entrepreneurs and even large corporations fail because they either think they're too busy or they're disinterested or just plain too disorganized to provide important and imperative follow-through calls. Whether they are a one-person company or a large organization, I guarantee they will eventually erode their own credibility and spiral downward. How do you prevent this from happening? Do the opposite of the failures! Follow through on each and everything you have promised. If you can't deliver as promised, then negotiate a new plan, but talk to them. Do it *now*, then make sure you *do* what you said you would do. Keep your finger on the pulse of your company's activities. Make absolutely sure you and your associates execute on following up and following through and success will be your partner. More on this in chapter 6...............

Who is your greatest competitor?

Whether you're a man shaving or a lady putting on her makeup, mornings have you looking into a mirror. Take a good look at your reflected image and study it very closely, Why? There in your mirror is your greatest competitor—*you!* Most people feel it has to be outside forces such as another similar company's associates cutting up your customer base or just other companies eroding your customers' disposable income. Maybe it could be Internet Web sites you feel are robbing you of past customers. These and many other factors could and may be a partial reason competitors are making it tough on you. *But no!* No, it's *you.* What you do every moment of the day is what separates you from any suspected competitors.

Is it a problem for you to get up early? Are you at your office first thing, or are other activities or engagements more important? Are you making that dreaded but all-important call today, or are you putting it off until tomorrow or the next day when it's more convenient? Are you completing the day by calling back every person who has called for you that day, or do you feel it can wait? Do you check your goals daily, or does this task get boring for you? Do you meet regularly with your associates to set direction, or do you not bother because you expect them to know? *Yes*, you are your own greatest competitor. Only you can make each step you take each day serve a special need, as no one else can do it for you. Understanding what *you* do every minute of each day is number one. Then you can assess what others are doing in your type of business and arrange your strategy to be a step ahead.

How do you put the pieces together?

It's imperative you have a complete grasp of your type of business. You then need key people working with you to participate in creating income, most especially income providing a solid profit. One method is to "share the wealth"—allow your associates to participate directly in their own production. You can enhance this by providing a system whereby you can have your associates sharing the wealth by receiving override income on top-flight new associates they recruit for your company. Override income allows for business associates and branch office managers recruiting new workers to receive a percentage of the company's portion of the new worker's commissions. When associates have a stake in the success of other producers, it helps build your firm. It also helps motivate associates to help others be successful as they share in the recruited person's success. Remember: if you can help your associates create wealth for themselves, they create wealth for you. It works!

Am I talking about pyramid schemes?

No way! I'm sure you have either read about or even been exposed to various schemes that claim they will make you an instant millionaire. You're asked to a special meeting in a place with nice aesthetics and presented this exciting opportunity whereby you sign up for certain products. You then are in a position to bring in new recruits to buy your products while in turn they bring in new recruits buying products—and it continues on and on. The idea is that if you're on top of that pyramid, you could have hundreds of people in an endless pyramid with you at the top drawing a percentage of everything each one sells. Who benefits? The company setting up the pyramid! You know the old saying, "If it sounds too good to be true, it usually is." In addition, pyramid schemes can be illegal.

However, when you have a company that requires each associate/salesperson to have a state or federal license, you may be able to set up a couple of tiers allowing you to obtain an override on new associates you've recruited. How's this done? You recruit a licensed associate who produces, and you then obtain an override on that new recruit. Those associates may then have an opportunity to manage their own company branch. In turn, the new branch manager brings in more licensed associates into that branch. You then obtain an override on those new people as well. Your company may then be able to allow your associates to participate in their own personal production plus two other tiers of new recruit production.

However, you may not have a continuous chain of overrides. Pyramid schemers would love to persuade you that there's no end to the percentage you receive on every new person brought in under your chain. **Unfortunately it's usually the people who organize and are at the Top of these pyramid programs that get the lump sum of wealth. Products are only sold to you as a new member. But instead** of you selling products in the retail market place it's your ability to enroll new pyramid members who are the only real buyers that make this scheme work. Eventually you as a new member end up buying your own product since you can't enroll any more of the diminished new members…it's a dead end! Beware of such claims and closely check out the company.

Why is a business needing licensing a better approach?

Remember, what we're after here is a way to Duplicate Yourself by working in a professional manner within an environment with licensed people. Licensing provides certain controls on how and what a producer can do. Consequently it prevents a new entrepreneur from getting carried away on attempts to "Duplicate Themselves" and cross over the line into illegal activity. Obtaining overrides on established associates plus on associates you've recruited allows you an exciting carrot: you are able to Duplicate Yourself and earn much more. In this type of structure, everyone can *share in the success* and *share in the wealth*!

Why is it best to get your own business started first before attempting to Duplicate Yourself?

You may start out just on your own, but if you expect to gain traction in a newly organized business structure, you need the synergy of key associates: people with like interests and experience in managing operations and knowledge as to how to recruit. It is absolutely *imperative* you have office management support, a "Mr. or Mrs. Inside," along with someone making sales and marketing contacts. (I call them a "Mr. or Mrs. Outside.") You need some type of mission statement or game plan laying out your course of action. To have a potential for future growth and overall success, you need to build an organization. Then you will be in a position to Duplicate Yourself.

How do you build an organization?

There's an old saying, "A company does not make people—people make a company." Again, the help of key people is imperative for enabling you to piggyback new ideas and providing support for carrying out those ideas. Support is critical, as human beings cannot flourish in a vacuum. Adding new people who may become key people provides illumination and synergy that in turn gives the extra punch allowing you to grow your organization.

What length of time can you expect to hold out when starting a new business operation?

I would advise having enough capital to get you through six months, but it's better if you can hold out for at least a year. After six months, take the first in-depth look at your experiment. If it has signs of life with some possible payback, then continue. Even if you're not sure, continue; however, after one year you should be able to get a feel whether it has any potential for success. If it looks promising, hang in there and continue to tinker with what works and experiment with additional angles that could become profitable. When you reach the end of your second year, take a good, solid, soul-searching appraisal of how it looks. If you're still borrowing from friends and relatives to keep your doors open, *stop*! Take your losses and new knowledge and move on. As they say, "Don't throw good money after bad." Quite often entrepreneurs let their pride get in the way of logical thinking. There's a reason another old saying holds true, "Pride cometh before the fall." Find a steady paycheck with a regular job and plan for the day you will try again.

What can family support do to cement confidence and growth?

As you are trying to get your new business off the ground, it's important to surround yourself with good people, those who are motivated and looking to create wealth with you as you grow your company. There's nothing like having a spouse or immediate family member involved with you. A spouse is a person very interested in your success, as your success is also your spouse's success. This holds true for other family members as well. If they're interested in working with you, they provide you support plus they protect your backside. It's exciting to have mutual goals tying them with you and your drive to make your business work. Having family members involved to help keep an eye on things may sound somewhat paranoid or harsh, but the realty is at the end of the day your associates go home where they deal with the goals and aspirations of their own household. Your spouse and family members stick with you and give you another set of eyes.

What other chapters can help tie together the special ingredients for success?

- **Chapter 5: Accumulate**
- **Chapter 9: The "Bloody Pulp" Theory**
- **Chapter 11: The Magic Power of Sharing**
- **Chapter 12: Universal Power**

Chapter 5

Accumulate

---------------------- $ ----------------------

How do you accumulate when you need every penny to survive?

As you move along with your new business, keep in mind the old saying that I will update a bit: "A hundred dollars *saved* is a hundred dollars *earned!*" It's almost impossible to accumulate during your start-up years when every dollar you earn is needed to keep you alive. However, make sure you do not tie yourself down to overhead costs just to have offices for show. **Instead find a small start up space, eliminate live receptionist cost with inexpensive and very effective Voice Mail Systems. Your Cell Phone can also be your first office, clients and prospects can reach you no matter where you are.** Save by keeping your new costs down any way and every way you can. This is imperative!!

Remember—the first of every month comes fast! Start out with as small a space as you can squeeze into. Buy secondhand furnishings and used copiers and fax machines. However, you do need a first-class computer and the latest programs. Go month to month on your rent until you see some cash build. As your income pie begins to increase, options will open up to you. Then you can look to step up, but I can't caution enough: A "big nut" (excessive ongoing monthly overhead costs) kills most start-up businesses. It's easy to understand why we get into this high overhead trap, as we all have our pride and egos. It's the urge to say "look at me—I have a successful operation," but as realty sets in, it becomes *"look at me—I'm in debt to my eyeballs."*

Can you leverage your way into business?

There's a big difference between looking for an opportunity within an existing business or corporate structure versus looking to purchase or start your own business from scratch. As an entrepreneur, you need a head start by acquiring working knowledge of how a particular business must work for you to succeed. If you have had experience, you have tremendous latitude. However, if you must rely on someone else's knowledge to set up your desired business, you're digging a hole for yourself. Why? Someone else will be calling the shots, and you must find a way of scraping up scarce upfront dollars to keep his/her expertise. In other words, you become the odd man or woman out!

Do not go into a new business venture expecting to *buy* your knowledge by hiring others, then learning on the job as you go along. Forget it! If you are bound and determined to start your own enterprise, pick your best shot—something with which you have specific experience with "sky is the limit" possibilities.

When you have a choice of purchasing an existing business versus leveraging your way in, I suggest you choose leveraging. Why? First, the cash down payment will eat up much needed start-up capital, plus borrowing means you must make payments on the debt that puts pressure on your monthly outlay. You bought a company based on its past client income thinking it would provide you guaranteed income, right? *Wrong!* Count on existing established competitors siphoning off your purchased company's clientele. There goes your expected cash flow, the money you expected to cover your monthly nut and keep you afloat while you build your purchased company. You end up paying for a disappearing asset. Don't do it—instead put your energy into starting from scratch. Starting from scratch works! Spend your limited resources on acquiring your own clients through advertising, family connections, your past connections, and former associates rather then being hobbled from day one by immediate debt. When you have working knowledge, this approach is great for small business start-ups! Remember, these things work if you work!

Can bringing in a partner help with your start up?

It's possible you may **choose to** start a small business with a partner. That means you can have two families contributing to start-up costs and ongoing costs of the new operation. Many partnerships work; however, a high percentage of these business partnerships end in the business equivalent of divorce, which results in a business dissolution. (I'll have more about this later on.) This can cause hardships and cut against successful continuation. Rather then enumerate all the positives and negatives of trying a partnership, let's move back to building on your own by surrounding yourself with first-class associates.

If you have knowledge, conviction, and motivation combined with a habit of doing "your thing," then you may be successful in bringing together a "mastermind" group of like-thinking associates. You can then be in a position to use the Duplicating Yourself Formula by allowing new top-notch associates to help you create and share the wealth. You will discover ideas supporting this approach throughout this endeavor.

How do you deal with your competition?

This has been discussed in an earlier chapter; however, redundancy can be good! A belief that seems to have much substance is that all things being equal, *you* are your only real competition. Take a good look in your morning mirror: what do you see? Does your mirror reflect a person with regular sleeping habits who is popping up most mornings ready to "hit it"? Do you see a person getting a head start on others in the same line of work,? A person having set and reviewed daily, weekly, and annual goals, who has repeated affirmations as to personal, family, and business goals? If this is the person you see, you're on your way to success. Write down and remember this old saying: *"First you make your habits; in the end your habits make you."* As many have said before, "life is a *journey,* not a *destination."* When this idea seeps into your subconscious mind, you can become more aware, confident, and happy about your daily journey. You are free from worrying about outside competition!

Make sure you set aside time in the morning and evening to mentally review your affirmations. Just a little application of time can do wonders. It doesn't have to be an hour or more as professed by some, but just five to ten minutes. This gives you a charge that in turn creates a steady flow of energy. You can then feel and understand an invigoration and power that carries you through each day, and yes, puts you in a class all your own. You can carry each day knowing the surge of positive energy steadily flowing through every fiber of your body will put you in the enviable position of standing above the crowd. Why? Because your habits carry the day! (More on affirmations in a later part of this chapter.)

Why should you run a "low cost, low nut" operation?

A tribute to any new business person is being able to "hang in" and see positive growth potential. Therefore *survival* is the name of your game! It's imperative to keep a "low nut," meaning you are keeping every conceivable cost as low as possible. Keeping your start-up costs down gives you two advantages:

1) **You give your new company a better chance to extend its business life and reach a break-even point.**

2) **You allow your company the opportunity for quicker profits that are not eaten up by large overheads— profit you can pass on to your new associates. Giving them more by sharing the wealth keeps them with you, plus newfound increased income becomes a catalyst to overall company morale and growth.**

How can independent contractors be used to advantage by keeping your "nut" down?

How sweet it is when most of the associates employed by your company can be considered independent contractors for IRS purposes. For example, a mortgage brokerage company in California is licensed under the State of California Department of Real Estate. All licensed loan agents must have an agreement with their individual or corporate mortgage broker, and this agreement can be designed as to make the agent an independent contractor. Licensed loan agents are essentially independent contractors in every practical sense. They control their own work time, pay for their own office space or work from their home, pay for their own equipment and transportation, provide their own medical insurance, pay their own taxes while receiving a 1099 from the mortgage company, etc. As I explain further, you will see that from the company's perspective, there is a huge advantage in this type of relationship.

What is the extra cost to you when covering employee payroll costs—and is there another way?

In a normal employer/employee relationship, the employer pays a salary to its employee. The employer withholds from the salary the employee's share of Social Security, then matches that contribution from its own funds. The employer must also pay various other federal and state employee taxes. In some cases, an employer also pays for part or all of the employee's medical insurance premiums. These costs place an employer in the position of paying an extra 25% to 30% over and above the employee's regular salary. If an employer also has an employee retirement program, costs may reach 40% of an employee's compensation. So an entrepreneur starting out and trying to build a small business is saddled with costs that could mean that for every dollar a business owner pays his employee, he has to add as much as another forty cents for their benefits. This is not to say the employees don't deserve it, but it merely illustrates the costs that may sink a start-up company.

Besides being hog-tied with salaries and benefit costs, how do you as a small business owner measure your employee's work effort in terms of your bottom line profit? It's practically impossible! And once a market slump occurs in your industry and revenues takes a dive, you are still faced with salaries comprising your biggest "nut." Here you are with your fixed costs for office rent, equipment leasing, etc.—plus having to continue salaries. You're faced with laying off most people or trying to hang in with them. Holding most of your employees is a humane thing to do, but it can also put you out of business. Working by yourself again versus paying employees may be much more than you can handle, so you are sitting on the horns of a dilemma where you're damned if you do and damned if you don't. What to do?

Thank goodness our American free enterprise system in some cases allows you to develop a business whereby most of your working associates are 1099'd and pay all of their own overhead costs and taxes, etc. This allows you as a start-up business two *big* advantages that can keep you in business. First, it takes pressure off of fixed monthly salaries and employee benefit costs. Second, you *do not* have to agonize as to whether your independent contractor is producing revenue. Independent contractors have to produce to sustain their own operations. If they are top producers, they can earn more as independent contractors than as salaried employees. The more the independent contractor earns, the more you as the entrepreneur owner earn from overrides on their production. It's a win/win situation. An additional advantage is if they do not or cannot produce, you're neither stuck with fixed salaries nor do you have to worry about terminating an employee. Lack of production that translates into lack of income takes care of the problem for you.

Essentially an independent contractor working with your company is a true partner. You both share a common interest. Revenues produced by the independent contractor provide a sustaining lifeblood by creating revenue shared by both parties. Yet during a cash drain in slower times, you're not stuck with a disabling fixed salary overhead; therefore, you can buy time without losing your business. Large fixed overhead expenses cause worry and anxiety that rob you of your positive energy and prevent you from moving forward. On the other hand, keeping those costs down enables you to cash in when our economy is running hot.

How do you know if your start-up business can use independent contractors? This is where prior research into your desired type of business provides an answer. Generally it's a type of business where an associate must have a state or federal license for specific type of work. But it could also be a business where workers with specialized training can telecommute and/or email product back and forth—think analysts, graphic designers, editors, or audio/video specialists. Make sure the independent contractors do control their own time and where they choose to operate and pay their own costs. An old IRS expression that determines whether a person is considered an independent contractor versus an employee is, "If it walks like a duck, quacks like a duck, and looks like a duck, then it is a duck!" This means that if person works in your office and you provide all the office overhead costs and expect certain set hours, etc., chances are that even if he/she is called an independent contractor and licensed and contracted by you, the IRS may consider that person a W-2 (salaried) employee instead of a 1099 independent contractor. Don't fall into this IRS trap. If your employee works away from office 51% of his/her work day, consider the use of a W2 Statutory Employee Agreement.

How can a mastermind motivational group help?

A mastermind motivational group is another of Napoleon Hill's concept's in *Think and Grow Rich*; it's a group of like-minded, like-thinking individuals getting together and creating and exchanging ideas. As you bounce ideas off each other, a magical thing can occur. For example, you throw an idea on the table, another piggybacks an idea off of your initial thought, then another adds to it, and so on.

Let's try an experiment with a flashlight to illustrate this concept. Take a large flashlight with three batteries, with each battery wired separately to a filament producing light. Then wire each battery directly to one another in series to the filament, and presto, you now have twice as much light! So it is with several minds kicking around ideas. Having two or more like-thinking minds can produce an incredible power allowing you to crystallize new and exciting ideas that you as an individual may never have considered.

How do you develop associates who help you accumulate wealth?

There's an expression, "Opposites attract, but likes stay together." It refers to a marriage relationship, but isn't any association a type of marriage? Many factors go into a long-term working relationship with one being developing associates with a similar philosophy regarding sharing ideas and giving back. You want associates who can explore ideas with you, present new ones, and become excited about coming up with new approaches to your company's opportunities to grow with their sharing in the wealth.

Associates who are not afraid to try something new should understand there may be a period of trial and error in determining whether an idea works. Remember the "it's just an experiment" concept found throughout this book. Creating a flexible organization with good like-minded people allows you to grow your company with excellent relationships providing positive energy. A synergy among good people creates an extra power very much like the extra power in our flashlight battery experiment. Through use of this power, wealth can be created and shared. As you evolve and grow with good people, they in turn will want to grow and share with you and continue a long-term, positive, and exciting working relationship of helping to accumulate wealth to be shared by all!

How does looking forward with goals versus worrying about the past create a faster path to accumulation?

Many start-up small businesses may fail because the key person—you—becomes bogged down with worry: worry about lost clients, associate relationships gone sour, and any and all things that sap your energy. How do you overcome this? Let me throw out a couple of ideas. First, you need to understand when you solve a problem, the solution becomes a potential new problem. As a good business owner/manager you need to understand you are in a problem-solving world. Managing your company is an art form in which to become successful, you must learn to be a first-class problem solver.

Setting goals is another critical part of putting current problems behind you and focusing on accumulating without going crazy. If you have goals set up for each week, each month, each year, and for five or even ten years ahead, and if you review these goals daily, they are planted in your subconscious mind where they stimulate and direct you to achieve them. I will have more on the subject of the subconscious mind and the magic of the universal consciousness in coming chapters. You begin to recognize problems are something you manage while your eyes are focused crystal clear with continued *success* as your main objective. You must recognize and take steps to solve each problem.

But remember: don't put your goals so high that you mentally break down when you don't come close to achieving them. Instead set your annual goals big enough to make you run to meet them, but where you still have a solid chance of reaching them. Talk about excitement and stimulation of reaching goals—there's nothing quite like it in the business world. Meeting goals catapults you to greater achievement by allowing you to develop confidence in your own planning and work ethic while inspiring your associates to stay with you. They know you can orchestrate a beautiful company symphony allowing for exciting opportunities for all to accumulate by creating and sharing the wealth.

How does a prosperity conscience help create and keep what you accumulate?

People have a prosperity conscience when they accept and appreciate their good fortune. This is the opposite of a poverty conscience where people feel they don't deserve their good fortune. There is a tough lesson to be learned here. Quite often you've gone through your learning and working years, then you start your second or third business enterprise and presto, a god in heaven shines down upon you. Your new enterprise is making you money, and lo and behold you begin to accumulate in a serious way. Be careful: do not allow yourself to fall into negative thinking by feeling you don't deserve your good luck. Quite often this comes from a poverty conscience in which you can't believe your good luck, so you worry about whether you really deserve it.

People who have had it tough worry about continuing to accumulate and are concerned about losing what they've built. They may unintentionally create a negative energy of fear that invades their subconscious mind. As a result, the very thing they fear most becomes realty. *Stop* this thinking. Hey, you worked hard, and you deserve all that's currently coming your way. Remember: millions of others have had varying degrees of success, including small business owners no more deserving than you. By focusing your thinking on how you can provide more for you and yours, keeping your money in circulation, and concentrating on continuing to build and share, guess what? Your world will expand and grow. Your prosperity conscience feeds positive energy into your subconscious, which in turn gives you a calm, warm, and fuzzy feeling that all is well with the world and that you are deserving.

How do past choices make you who you are today?

I believe it's obvious Deepak Chopra, author of *The Seven Spiritual Laws of Success*, has had quite an influence on me. As I read his book, I was amazed how intimately I shared his beliefs. When I finished it, I summarized some of its lessons to myself in this way: "Essentially you *are* what you have *done* every day prior to this one. Every choice you have made intentionally or even subconsciously, remember if it's subconsciously, you may not realize it was a choice. But regardless, those choices create what's happening to you now." Consequently if you did well in past ventures but eventually failed, it may be because your choices (conscious or not) took you down the wrong path. This means you need to condition yourself to think in a different mode. One way is to study carefully the previous choices you've made and their consequences. As you engage in making a critical choice, three areas of your physical body react: your brain/mind, your heart, and your gut. It seems your gut (as in gut-level feeling) needs to be understood the most. If your choice makes you feel lousy, there you are; if your gut gives you a feeling of calmness, there it is!

Current and future choices: how do you understand them?

Remember, every single choice you have made and are currently making is who you are this minute! Do you wonder how siblings all brought up in the same household may look alike and even have similar mannerisms, yet be so different as they grow into adulthood?

I believe your gene mix is your dominant force. You can be taught and nurtured, but something all-pervasive seems to drive our psyche, leading us to temptation rather than accomplishment. However, you can't stand back and say, "Well it's my ancestors' genes in me—I can't help myself." Bull! That's a pure and simple copout, a life crutch. Yes, you may be inclined to take an easy way out, but it must be fought. Those of you fortunate enough to feel comfortable in each choice you make can be thankful. Others of you have to work much harder to develop and stay on the higher plane that can lead you to happiness and success in life.

To my knowledge, there is no science that if you follow it exactly, you can be assured of a perfect life. You and me as individuals are extremely complex. Medical researchers and psychologists continuously research and investigate in order to learn more about our nature. You merely have to understand why all your prior choices have placed you on a higher plane to ultimate success; however, if you haven't achieved success, then study any choices leading to failure. We must either learn from our past errors or be subject to repeating them again and again. Our next chapter deals with results from inspiration, perspiration, and compensation and how they work hand in hand with execution.

Chapter 6

Execution–The Key to Business Success

——————————— $ ———————————

CYCLE OF SUCCESS: "INSPIRATION, perspiration, compensation." I enter this chapter by attempting to show a common denominator found as an inextricable key to successful operations—that is, *execution*! I will explore a number of insights that may help you along your path. There is an exciting combination of words defining the beginning, middle, and end to a well-executed business plan: *inspiration, perspiration,* and *compensation.*

Inspiration   Perspiration   Compensation

Inspiration **is all of your exciting combinations of ideas igniting a start to your new business.**

Perspiration **is your intensive work and effort as you move along with your business plan.**

Compensation—**ah, compensation is an exhilarating completion of hard work: your *pay* day.**

These three words form a complete cycle, with success being the execution of this cycle over and over again.

EXECUTION:

In business, *execution*, if improperly done, can literally mean the death of your company, but if used as defined here, it will be its life. There's no question that inspiration, perspiration, and compensation creates a cycle of initial thought, then hard work, finally leading to being paid and making a profit, but during this process you must execute if you are to become a successful operation. What do I mean by execution?

Follow Up

- Make sure you get back to customers, clients, and associates by day's end.
- Angry clients must be called ASAP whether you have answers or not.
- Meet with your associates weekly, **making sure execution of each one these items is done.**

Follow Through:

- Your word is your bond; make sure you complete all commitments made.
- If you can't deliver on the date agreed, call the client ahead of time and explain.
- Zeroing in on your associates and their following through is your company's life.

I'll provide more information on the way execution can be accomplished through follow up and follow through as you continue reading.

Is franchising a good idea or a waste of time?

Quite often start-up businesses have in their business plan a desire to franchise themselves as soon as they have a modicum of success. McDonald's and Burger King as well as Kentucky Fried Chicken are just a few of the incredible stories of riches achieved by these and many other franchisers. It seems to me unique retail operations are those most likely to evolve into successful franchise operations. So it depends on your product. In our examples above, we're dealing more in the realm of sales organizations. However, I don't want to rule out anything you may want to attempt, as after all, I do believe "the sky's the limit."

Are you afraid others may see your successful business plan and copy it?

In this chapter, I will review the concept that if you build an exciting, profitable start-up business, others may want to emulate your success causing you worry and anguish on how to protect your business operation. I say don't worry—and I will explain why. My advice is not to start out with grandiose ideas of franchising, at least not until you have a firm grasp of executing a business plan with some success. Execution of your business operation is a key to fortune, something that will be explained as I go along.

A business plan is only as successful as your team of associates and your own ability to execute the plan. Consequently, you should spend less time being concerned about someone discovering your plan. It means nothing: it's your basic personal and business philosophy and the way you're able to lead appropriately that counts. One hundred different people could take your complete business plan and interpret it in a hundred different ways. Once you show success, imitators will pop up. Don't go crazy over it—followers are just imitators who have no clue as to how your personal philosophy and leadership makes your operation a winner.

How can you avoid being "poured in concrete"?

Again I bring up an expression used by a former associate of mine (and no, his name wasn't Soprano). As you move into your new start-up business, don't allow yourself to take fixed positions or get bogged down or trapped into a stated position, one you feel you have to take to survive and thrive. Instead you must allow room for change and maneuverability. The U.S. Constitution is a good example of a document that allows additions as they become necessary as our country grows and changes. Fortunately our Founding Fathers saw fit to provide opportunities for future amendments. So you to must be prepared to back off and institute changes when stumbling blocks impede your progress. It's human nature to hang on to what you consider to be *the* way—the only way. No one wants to lose face. Yet I repeat, call your business plan an experiment so you have a psychological edge if wholesale changes must be made or you must stop and go in a new direction.

How can experimenting make your business plan successful?

Calling a business plan an experiment may have various connotations for different people. Years ago, my little but dynamic company wanted to recruit someone to be in charge of a growing region in Southern California. We found a gentleman with experience in our industry who also had a terrific background with a political group. Along with being an advisor on fifty-nine political campaigns in Southern California, he had a distinguished run as a deputy assistant to the Director in the Small Business Administration in Washington DC during the Reagan administration. Now he was back in private practice. We outlined a plan for him as to the way he could manage a regional operation for our firm. We explained to him how our firm believed in sharing the wealth, and that as he helped us grow our southern region, he'd directly participate in the wealth created. As our meeting was ending, we described to him our concept of our plan being an experiment. He hesitated, then said, "I'll get back to you." What we didn't understand was in government work, an experiment was something short-term, and when the grant money was gone, so was your position.

Once we understood, we used our Motherland, the good old USA, as our analogy, explaining this country of ours has been evolving as an "experiment" for 225 years. He came aboard, and we had great success with him as a key member of our team. Later when we would review a new plan as an experiment, he'd give us a small, understanding smile. He knew that even if we had to stop or change directions, we would still 'be' in it for the long haul!

As you are cranking up your new enterprise, it's important to push hard on what does work. In other words, accentuate the positive. Conversely, dead end results need to be reviewed carefully; when you feel hamstrung, reject them and head in a new direction with never a look back! "Experimenting" is a good thing.

Why is copying you a form of great flattery?

There are times when a small business start-up has a certain level of success, then suddenly you see would-be competitors using all or part of your game plan. Don't worry, and don't get mad—in fact don't bother to get even. Imitation is a great form of flattery! You are making it happen your way, and as your competitors are taking notice, you're doing something right. Continue to work at it using your keen sense of execution and watch your imitators fall by the wayside. However, even if they succeed with your system, that's fantastic, as good karma always comes back to you.

Believe it or not, good can come out of your competition taking over your ideas. It gives you an excellent opportunity to do some investigative work of your own and determine if there are areas where you might tweak your plan, whether it may be in recruitment, commission plans, products available, etc. and get a jump ahead on those would-be competitors. Remember, success breeds imitation. **You will find competitors may 'piggy back' on your business plans by offering an even more 'cutting edge' advantage. Fine! You can then turn around** and steal their **new ideas for your company, turn around is fair play, right?**. However, your biggest reason to not fear is what I will go into next. If you have nailed down execution of your game plan, no one—I mean no one—is going to outdo you. So don't fear imitators: merely steal back their tricks and continue on your exciting path to financial accumulation as you share the wealth!

Game plan execution: How did Coach Vince Lombardi "win, baby, win"?

It's possible you've reached a point where you're starting to get sick of my continual insistence on executing your plan. I understand! But I must continue to hammer away on this issue. Why? Because there's nothing more critical, and if done correctly you have your *key* to eternal business success. For those of you who enjoy sports and have some knowledge of sports history, let's illustrate execution in Coach Lombardi style.

In 1959, Vince Lombardi was hired on by Green Bay, Wisconsin, to coach a former professional football powerhouse team nicknamed the Green Bay Packers. Green Bay was looking to rebuild to its former glory days. Although Green Bay was a small market area with extremely cold winters, at age forty-five Vince Lombardi accepted this new position as an exciting midlife challenge. Green Bay was also looking to fill the general manager's position, but when Lombardi showed up, he told them, "I want it understood I'm in charge here." Two days later he was given the general manager's job as well (see the PACKERS.com Web site).

In his first season, he was named Coach of the Year and barely missed a national championship. In his second year, he turned his team into a perennial national champion, winning big year after year. Then in 1967 he won the first national championship called Super Bowl I followed in 1968 by his winning Super Bowl II. Coaches around the NFL took special notice of Lombardi's successful offensive style of play. Many NFL coaches felt all they needed to do was carefully scout all of Lombardi's games and break down his offensive plays, then presto—by imitation and their own superior athletic talent. they would beat Lombardi at his own game, right? *Wrong!*

What they didn't realize was Lombardi's need for perfection. His style of offense was very simple, nothing like the complex systems being innovated then by other teams that have continued into our current era. His offense was so basic as to be transparent to any scout, coach, or fan. It went something like this: on running plays, he pulled the left guard, then left tackle who swept to the right along with the fullback and a halfback along with the center, guard, tackle, and end on the right side of his line. They would all block for their quarterback who handed off to his other halfback, who in turn ran for several yards over blocked and confused defensive backs. When running to the right gained fewer than three yards, Lombardi would do the same thing going to his left side. As defensive backs tightened up and sucked in to prevent runs, his quarterback faked a run, stepped back, and threw a touchdown pass to a streaking wide receiver with no one within forty yards of him! Ridiculous, you say?

Any coach could figure out Lombardi's style in a moment, so why was he so successful? *Execution, execution, execution!* Lombardi would spend hours going over each minute step and movement by each lineman and back. Over and over again he would have them run each play until he reached near perfection. Blistered and exhausted players were cajoled, motivated, and inspired to repeat each play again and again. Even in their sleep, his players would be dreaming about each step and each move. While awake, they dreaded Lombardi's wrath if his style of perfection wasn't achieved. Every pro team knew exactly how each of Lombardi's plays worked, but they couldn't stop them. Coaches throughout the NFL tried his style of offense, yet couldn't beat Lombardi's Packers. Why? He excelled in executing each play perfectly. He didn't care if they found his playbook. Again why? He knew no one could *execute* his plays better than his own athletes. Their minds, hearts, and souls had each play perfectly ingrained into their subconscious. Next let's illustrate a few points absolutely imperative for your own start-up business's success.

How does "follow up and follow through" make a complete difference?

Have you ever run into associates, clients, friends, or vendors who when you request them to take a specific action, answer something like "no problem" or "forget it—it's done"? Then time goes by, and not only have they not responded to your request or completed what you asked them to do, but they haven't bothered to advise you of anything at all. I hope this is a pet peeve of yours; it certainly is one of mine. On top of that, days, weeks, or months after your request, if you run into these same people on the street, they'll say, "Hey, I've been trying to get a hold of you." Does this get you? Can you feel smoke coming out of your ears?

Follow up is absolutely essential to developing credibility with your peers, customers, or associates. Don't let twenty-four hours go by without giving people requesting info their reply. If it's bad news, let them know right away. Don't hold off—it only gets worse. If you don't have an answer, call them anyway. Why? They're anxious to hear, and not advising them because you don't know doesn't ease their anxiety, it only increases it. They need to know you're keeping them in the loop, something that's not only appreciated but necessary in building the bridges leading to ultimate and continued success.

But following up is only part of an equation that makes a difference in relationships. *Follow through* is your second half of making a difference. Have you ever requested associates or others to take a specific requested action, and when you asked them about their progress, they said, "I'm working on it—I'll get back to you"? They don't give you a time line, just leave you hanging. How does this sit with you? Maybe at first you're able to roll with it, but when it happens time after time, then what?

Likewise when clients or customers request something specific of you, it's imperative to advise them when they can expect a completed job. Then keep them posted in a timely way and deliver their goods on time. If it can't be completed or delivered on time, notify them immediately. Excuses are killers, especially after they are given to your client/customer only after repeated calls to you.

A combination of follow up and follow through creates a climate for your success. Look around at people you know who are successful in any type of business or sales. If you dig in to what makes them tick, you'll find it's their main ability to follow up and follow through that has helped them in building a successful operation. Credibility is the name of the game! Generally although you need cash assets to start your business, your greatest contribution is your ability to follow up and follow through.

Why does hammering away and being redundant create credibility?

It's quite possible repeating instructions or information to associates, clients, customers, or vendors gets on their nerves. However, all too frequently they fail to understand completely what must be done.

How often have you heard, "Hey, that isn't what you told me?" Even when you answered, "Yes, it was!" arguing who's right doesn't solve your problem. Getting it done does! So, tell 'em once, tell 'em twice, fax 'em, e-mail 'em, etc.!

Communication is a two-way street. You must communicate your request to your listener. In turn your listener must understand your message, then respond with an understanding of that message. I will add, "A lack of understanding of communications causes headaches." Repeating your communication as part of your follow-up is imperative. I can go a step further: you may have a situation where you've communicated your request and/or thoughts to people, and they have responded in a way that allows you to feel comfortable. However, all along what they thought you said and what you thought they said wasn't what anyone thought. Has this ever happened to you? Translations can get warped in our attempt to communicate an idea, request, or thought. Being redundant can be good.

Why must you say what you do and do what you say?

Have you ever had people sincerely tell you what they were going to do for you, then change it in midstream? You were set to expect something—it was a promise, not an experiment or proposal requiring flexibility. You were set on that something being exactly what your someone advised you it would be. Then upon delivery of what was promised, all was changed. How did you feel? Exactly as any associate, customer, or client would feel if you pulled this on them. If you want to build a successful company, you must have *credibility*. And credibility comes from laying it on the line and doing what you said you'd do. There are times when you may get burned on a deal by getting shortchanged, but in the long run, people will believe in you and rally around you. If you promise something to someone, you'd better back it up. If you mouth it, do it!

When is it beneficial to call a business change of direction an "experiment," and why?

As I talked about in the previous paragraph regarding saying what you'll do and doing what you say, you may think the advice now being offered is contradictory. *No!* Calling something an experiment immediately puts everyone on notice so they understand you're dealing with flexibility. This means you may discontinue your plan, you may change your plan, and you may redirect your plan. When is it beneficial to call a business change in direction an experiment? Right away, as soon as planned, so you're giving fair notice. It's important people you work with understand and are in concert with your thinking. Anytime people show skepticism concerning your experimental approach, remind them of our U.S. Constitution. It has been a continual experiment for 225 years and continues as one into our foreseeable future.

Why must technology be used to perfect execution?

Even though old-timers like me have a problem being on top of the hi-tech curve, knowledge and understanding of its uses is an absolute must. In fact, in some cases Third World countries have jumped ahead of international economic powers in hi-tech use. Why? These countries couldn't afford to provide the infrastructure of landline phones or most twentieth-century communications systems. However, because of satellites, etc, these countries have made a leap into our twenty-first century with cell phones and widespread incorporation of wireless Internet access, etc. Efficient communication is a must, so you should continually maximize your use of any latest technology to give your company an edge in speed while giving you a leg up in executing your business plan.

Would you like a quick history of how technology improved the bottom line?

Running a successful company means balancing the cost and efficiency of your support staff with production and your bottom line. Use of high-tech equipment has changed the face of our American workforce. Circa the 1980s, a movie came out called *Nine to Five*. In one scene, the audience observed a sea of ladies working on row after row of IBM Selectric typewriters. These typewriters were state of the art then, as they even gave the user the ability to erase an error on a typed page by typing over it using the correcting ribbon. Wow! However, within fifteen years of that movie, Selectric typewriters had become antiques. Computers were what you saw on each desk. Bosses, male or female could then use computer programs to do most of the work formerly done by a huge support staff. Consequently computers represented considerable savings to a small business operation, one that could ultimately turn a break-even operation into a profitable one.

How does associate accountability insure execution of your business plan?

One way is to provide weekly meetings—not just bull sessions, but meetings with some teeth. During them you must request specific information from each of your key people. Lay it out in a formal agenda. Touch on each particular job: what is expected, and where your associate is on meeting that particular objective. Do this in group meetings. Why? Group meetings accomplish several things. First, it allows each member of your key team to know what others are doing so there's no overlapping. Two, it creates a little adrenaline action in members of your key team, as everyone is listening to whether people have done their jobs. Three, it allows those who feel they've done good work to express their positive thoughts and feel good about themselves. This provides greater communication and accountability between associates and sets forth an organized way to effective execution of your current business activities.

How do you obtain current reports from key associates?

Let's assume you have a weekly meeting with your key associates. Provide them with an agenda a full day before your meeting. This gives them a chance to make their follow-up calls and provide you with up-to-date information. Next morning, hand out an update of your agenda. This forces busy associates to make final preparations for your key team meeting.

At your meeting, **help everyone visualize** what you currently want accomplished and why. Make sure everyone's on your same page of keeping your company goals alive. Discuss their replies in detail, and make sure they understand they're a critical part of your team. Listen to feedback from your team, as quite often it reveals a better way. Follow your agenda, but avoid creating a tense atmosphere; allow your associates to speak out and act up. It's important to provide a positive give-and-go so your meetings can be enjoyed by your associates.

How do you counter and act when reports are not received and you're in the dark?

An interesting way is to place subtle peer pressure on your key associate during your meeting. Here's a possible scenario: all of your key associates are meeting with you (this could be two or four or six associates). In your prior meeting, an associate was asked about a particular task; the associate's response was, "I forgot to follow up on it." This week you ask your associate the same question, and the associate looks around at the other associates and meekly replies, "I forgot, but I'll get right on it." How do you think this associate will handle your same question next week? **I do believe your associate will be inspired to save face and get the answer for the next meeting. However, if this person persists in not following up again and again they put themselves in a position of "saving face or facing exit"!**

How to be accountable and avoid treating associates like "growing mushrooms?

Imagine that you work in the lower decks of an ocean liner as an engine mechanic. You haven't been given any information on your liner's destination. You're only accountable to keep those engines running twenty-four hours a day. **Since you also live** below decks **you have no clue as to what's happening on the rest of the ship.** Are you a happy camper? What's your attitude?

Let's take this same example and change our facts slightly. Once a week, your captain and ship's officers meet with you and all department heads responsible for operating this liner. They outline every facet of your journey, your current destination, weather, etc. They even let you topside to check out the view. How do you feel now?

I'm sure you're aware of how to grow mushrooms: *"You keep them in the dark, then feed them lots of horse manure."* That may be a good way to grow mushrooms, but with human beings this approach is deadly. An absolute is to make everyone in your organization understand your firm's journey and destinations and their role in reaching them.

Your associates need to know how their small part contributes to your company's success. Being a part of something successful and sharing in the wealth based on each associate's contribution lends to a healthy, positive work environment. Out of darkness comes light, and accountability becomes exciting if not automatic.

Chapter 7

Peanuts Attract Monkeys

—————————— $ ——————————

Why do "peanuts attract monkeys" in the workplace?

A close relative of mine owned a garbage service. As his business grew, he became more and more agitated about his drivers: "My help is tearing up my trucks. They strip transmissions, blow out tires by running over curbs, miss work. I'm going crazy. On top of that, they're too lazy to work so I'm constantly training new replacements. When new drivers take over, they miss garbage stops, causing daily complaints, plus they continue to tear up my equipment. I'm definitely going nuts!"

I once went to a marketing seminar regarding personnel. One speaker suggested, "Call up your office, muffle your voice, and ask for yourself—then see what happens." Everyone laughed. But before voice mail became acceptable, a receptionist handled incoming calls. We'd all experienced dropped connections, the wrong person getting our call, etc. He asked us, "Why does a multimillion dollar organization pay the least amount to the first person a customer talks to? Your company image hinges on first impressions, correct?"

Point well taken. Then he explained how owners of companies paying entry-level wages with minimal benefits and long waits for a pay raise complained about their inability to keep good people long-term. These company owners/managers didn't have a clue as to why their company was a revolving turnstile for employees. Our speaker then advised on how to eliminate this problem: "Pay above industry averages, pay for benefits, reward those doing more with pay increases, and provide profit-sharing incentives. Make those with positive attitudes and exuberant energy managers or assistant managers over other employees." He then added. "Remember, it costs more money to constantly interview, hire, and train new personnel than giving good people top money and keeping them. A key is to keep good people over the long haul. This eliminates ownership's biggest harassments: downtime costs of retraining, and anxiety over the day-to-day needs to get a job done correctly. *Peanuts Attract Monkeys*."

When I went back to my relative who had the garbage service and asked him what he paid his employees, he became instantly enraged and snarled, "I pay top dollar—as much as they get at 'Travel Accessories' across town."

I held my ground and mentioned that "Travel Accessories" employees worked in an air-conditioned environment plus had retirement benefits, sick leave, and paid vacation time. He responded, "It makes no difference—you can't depend on lazy SOBs." I was working for an insurance company at that time, and I asked him to listen to me as I might have some suggestions to help keep his sanity. I explained what I had learned at my marketing seminar.

He said he'd listen but his expression was disdainful—like someone biting into a lemon. I explained to him that maybe he should do more to keep these people. He shouted, "I pay them too damn much now!"

"Okay," I said, but suggested he try this: "Set up a little pension plan for anyone sticking with you for six months or more. Pay their health insurance benefits. Set up a paid vacation plan. Have your best driver help run your Truck Shop, make him dispatcher, and give him a raise." By golly he listened and began putting a plan to work.

Six months later I was visiting with him. He had this big smile and said, "You know, little brother, I thought you were full of crap. But my tire, engine, and transmission repair bills have gone down more than the cost of those benefits. I'm now hanging onto some good workers, and I think I'm regaining my sanity!" Just remember that *peanuts attract monkeys!*

How can you avoid creating a revolving door atmosphere with company associates?

If you're running a sales organization, you need to set up a system where top producers are rewarded with higher commissions. Top commission sales people are much like top professional athletes: they love you and want to be loyal, but "show me the money" is their hue and cry. Maintaining top producers is essential to maintaining a first-class field force. If you've lost good people, take a good look at what your commission percentage is to them, as their loyalty to you depends greatly on what you pay them.

Other factors are important to retaining good people. Commission people work hard for their commission checks. They don't like a company playing around by delaying or holding back their earned commission money. "Pay fast, pay quick" gains their everlasting appreciation of you. Another factor is having excellent products for your sales force. Just as an archer needs more specialty arrows in his quiver to shoot, they need more terrific products in their arsenal to push. Plus whether your employees are on salary or independent contractors, it's great to have the synergy of good people around them. Providing top and speedy pay, competitive products, and recognition as part of an exciting team helps maintain first-class associates who in turn help you grow an outstanding organization.

Peanuts attract monkeys! $$$ attract and keep top people!

How do you compare a team of horses with "yes men"?

If you understand this question, you're a step ahead of me. You've probably heard plenty about how "yes men" can place a company at a disadvantage. Why? They feel if they cross the boss by suggesting alternate ideas, the boss will get sick of them, so they refuse to dissent, consequently shutting out potentially good ideas for company growth. All of this is true, but there's another side: disruption.

I remember as a kid that my father used four horses to pull loaded hay wagons. Harnessed horses were chained to one another with harness straps and wooden hitches allowing our horses to evenly pull their load. But there was one frisky horse on Dad's team. Things got tough when our four horses had to pull hard up a steeper grade. Our frisky horse would buck, pull to one side or another, and completely disrupt our team's efforts to get over the hill. Once Dad replaced the frisky horse with one that kept in step, all hills were easily topped. In a business, a constantly dissenting voice also disrupts a company team trying to plan, experiment, and project ideas for the company's growth and well-being. As the old saying goes, you can't let a bad apple spoil the barrel. It's important to be surrounded by associates who can ask hard questions, but still help supply exciting solutions. Pulling together as a team creates synergy that catapults everyone in a positive, winning direction.

Why does like-minded thinking create the best synergy?

At one time I had an associate full of terrific ideas, but unfortunately most of them were moving in a direction other than where most of my other associates felt we needed to go. Consequently most of his ideas were shot down. One day he jumped me about it, angrily saying, "You don't want to just be surrounded by 'yes men' do you?" My first reaction was to say no, of course not. However, as I thought it through, it became clear having constant opposition and resistance to most of the ideas my associates were brainstorming could be a downer. Sometimes an associate was critical of an idea that most associates were excited about trying. Although it's important to leave room for piggybacking new thoughts, someone constantly shooting down ideas without reciprocating with alternate thoughts stems the flow and kills the energy that might come up with a better way. Maybe it's time for those particular associates to use their strong ideas to start and run their own company. In contrast, there's no question like-minded thinking allows piggybacking of ideas in a positive atmosphere, thereby providing winning solutions.

Why do two or more minds working together create much more then the sum of their parts?

One person may have an idea, and possibly he/she will write it down, observe, and analyze it. When two people are together, one may have an idea, and while that person is analyzing it, another may be struck by a spin-off thought springing from the original idea. When three or more people are kicking around ideas, a shared enthusiasm develops. These several people create off of one another, and as excitement builds, new inspiring ideas come forth that may be put to immediate use. Several minds working in concert can usually do much more then any one of these minds working on its own. But try telling that to Albert Einstein, huh?

How far must you go to influence someone to join your efforts?

Whether you are presenting a plan to your current associates or trying to influence someone to join your organization, certain criteria must be adhered to for achieving a successful outcome. First of all, you must know your plan has teeth—positive ideas that can work and greatly benefit your company. If it's someone you're trying to bring aboard, then make sure you know all you possibly can about that person before making your pitch.

Present your plan in a well-laid out, easy-to-read and understandable format. Highlight your best points to make them stand out and be easily seen and understood. When you sit down in your meeting or recruit interview, make sure you look well groomed, smell good, and look good. If this is your first meeting with someone, an old saying about first impressions is in order: "First impressions are the most lasting."' Finally, give it your best shot. At times being excited and enthusiastic about your idea or your company carries more weight and is more convincing than plain, raw facts. There's something to another old saying, "Enthusiasm makes the difference."' It's amazing how someone showing tremendous enthusiasm can imbue all those around with passion and excitement, helping them to accomplish what might have seemed impossible.

Why does going "too far over the line" create a negative effect?

Has it ever happened to you that you're working hard to persuade someone to join your organization when you reach a point where compensation becomes a point of contention? You find yourself giving away more and more and getting less and less. Next, the person must think about it. You continue your aggressive campaign by calling, e-mailing, or faxing new and exciting information. You've actually gone far beyond the evenhanded deal first extended to them, but the person wants more. What do you do now? I believe the following bears repeating:

Here's an idea of how you should philosophically approach these types of situations. Consider your negotiations as if there were a fence between you and your potential recruit (or it could be anyone with whom you're trying to establish a relationship). This fence is where you have an imaginary line between both of you. That fence represents a midpoint where you feel both parties need to meet to consolidate your new relationship—call it meeting halfway. If you have to extend your body over your imaginary fence to grab your prospect and force him/her to your midpoint, you have a shaky deal. If you have to jump over your fence and pull the other person to middle ground, you don't have a deal. Do not continue to chase the person. Don't go crazy over it—just drop it, turn your back, and walk away. When two parties each feel great about meeting halfway, if it's done with sincerity, and your intuition is positive, chances are excellent you've got a deal.

What must a potential new associate have and know about your operation to be successful?

I believe a story is in order to give you a glimpse into the recruitment of new associates and how my firm has gotten a chuckle out of what a new associate might expect from us. Our company depends on continually acquiring new first-class professional associates via newspaper ads, direct mail, and e-mail. Our most successful method is word-of-mouth referrals from our branch managers and current happy and productive associates. As previously mentioned, our business is primarily a sales organization with people coming aboard as independent contractors. (Although the Labor department is getting tougher on this status, they prefer your people being paid as salaried W2 employees.)

These independent contractors are quite often associates on a commission plan. These are top professionals who know how to market for their own customers. They hold appropriate state licenses and have both intricate knowledge and experience in our business and a track record of solid production. Essentially our company wants associates who have paid the price for their success and now wish to have a top commission plan.

But frequently when prospects reply to our ads, all we get out of it is a good laugh. The scenario goes like this: Our company recruiter conducts interviews. Our prospects then advise what *they* want. They want to be trained, they admit they don't have required licenses, they need to be given leads, and last but not least, they must have a salary draw.

Our recruiter politely tells them, "When you find a company that will do all of this, give me a call—I'll go to work for them ASAP!" Of course our company recruiter doesn't leave them holding an empty bag, as prospects are advised of companies that do specialize in training and licensing. But for a company to do all this, they must pay only a low commission. Such companies always need middle management who must be compensated for training new agents by taking a percentage of those agents' earned commission. Our recruiter tells them that once they have gotten their license, been trained, built a body of clients, and established a successful track record, they should please call us as we'll give them an instant raise!

As part of initial interviewing, when you sense your callers may be good prospects, it's important to get as much information as possible from them. What do they expect? Are they interested in working on their own or in a branch office? Would they like to run their own branch and bring in new associates? Then we proceed to lay out all options available to them and determine if we can make a fit. Finally, their hot button issue is what they want their commission percentage to be. Depending on their past six months' production at their prior job and whether they want to open their own branch office, we can provide them an industry-leading commission plan. Or we can offer a top commission package based on a monthly production bonus plan.

Is there a way to be independent and yet be part of a group?

Every once in awhile I have to pinch myself. My father was a Portuguese citizen from the Azores Islands (nine tiny islands in a mid–Atlantic Ocean archipelago). He was given U.S. citizenship by serving two years in World War I. He then returned to the Azores, married my mother, and brought her to America where they raised a family of five with me as the middle child.

Think about this: being born in a country that became a premier world economic and superpower, then being raised in California, the richest U.S. state. Wow! America's incredibly successful free enterprise system is envied by all, with some hating us for having it. A Communist government in Germany built a wall to *keep people in*, while our USA is in a mess today *trying to keep people out*. Why are millions of illegal/undocumented aliens trying to force their way in? For opportunity and a better life for them and their family. Like other Western democracies, the American entrepreneurial system does allow business opportunities where you don't have to reinvent the wheel, as you can be part of an organization allowing you to operate as a wheel within a wheel.

These opportunities are available through various setups such as running a franchise operation. A corporation owns certain things, but you can operate your unit as your own boss within certain production limits. Or you can purchase your own unit within a franchise concept and be your own boss. Sales organizations quite often lend themselves to your being an independent contractor and running your own branch office with a sales organization providing you with licensing and all the products you need to *win*! Successful firms generally have a company philosophy outlining how they feel about their field force and their client/customer relationships as well as "sharing in the wealth" and long-term commitments to you. They want to see if you believe in how they operate and to determine the way you may interact with their company's offerings. If you see a fit, give it a shot!

How far can and should you go in building a team of like-minded associates?

Let's assume you have some knowledge of sports teams. Even if you don't, can you imagine a group of athletes being highly successful if they all had their own ideas and methods on how to win? That being said, it's still imperative to have a team of associates who are sharp and highly motivated and may have their own ideas. However, attitudes make a big difference. While new associates may have their own mindset as to how to make things work, they must still be willing to listen and learn. A key is to have new associates with past success willing to work your system. There's nothing more stimulating and successful than like-minded people. These people have no need to constantly bicker and play devil's advocate as to ideas presented them. Rather they are too busy piggybacking ideas and developing new ways to make things happen within a tried-and-proven system presented to them.

You must go all the way when recruiting your new people, which means you should make every effort to bring people into your organization with open minds, positive attitudes, willingness to learn, and motivation to succeed. Chances are they will then be associates willing to stick together and grow together. Harmony is good, as harmony helps create an atmosphere conducive to growth. As success involves a synergistic explosion of energy that infuses your group, all can benefit when there's no bad apples to spoil the barrel.

Why is a business partnership essentially a marriage?

As Steve Martin might say, "Duh, you think?" It is a *marriage!* Even if it's not a marriage contract, a business partnership contains all the ingredients of a marriage. For example, covering your partner's back is essential. Talking over all issues involving day-to-day and organizational concepts is also important, as is having a basic understanding of ongoing business decisions.

Mutual respect between partners is important to begin with and needs to be nurtured if a solid, successful relationship is to evolve. When differences of opinion arise—and they will arise—it's imperative to step away from others involved in management and support staffing. Put your heads together and brainstorm solutions to your differences. If the matter concerns irrevocable decisions made by a party that may have had a negative impact on the company, time must be taken to lay out all specifics. When operating in a full disclosure type of partnership environment, chances are much greater that disputes will be resolved amicably. Having one or more partners sharing a basic philosophy with a like-thinking approach to their business and personal lives helps create the truly successful business marriage.

When does a married couple prosper from their relationship in business?

How often have you heard a husband or wife say, "There's no way we can work together!" If they really mean it, there's not much of a remedy available. However, what usually gets on a couple's nerves is when both parties are doing the same things within the business, or in other words, splitting similar duties. This can become a problem simply because each person may have his/her own way of getting a job done. People may drive their partner crazy as to how they go about doing the job and how long it takes to get final results. How can this be changed to make their work compatible?

If each one does something different within the business operation, chances become exponentially greater that a happy and fruitful relationship can evolve. For example, one person may handle the bookkeeping and ordering while the other takes care of public relationships and personnel. There are many combinations of divided work each spouse may be able to do separate from one another. Separate contributions provide for a better team effort and allow each spouse a bit of pride for his/her own efforts. However, there must be a give-and-go by each party as they plug along to make sure all bases are covered. It's important when each spouse is motivated by the operation; it's got to feel good, which means it must be a natural thing for each one. Spouses also need to work within their strengths, as doing so makes work much easier. When there's common goals, a feeling for their business, and working within each person's respective strengths, great and exciting things will happen for a married couple working together. It works, believe me!

JUST THE FACTS

Happiness is ...

89% of entrepreneurs report being involved in a happy marriage or relationship.

Of those, 85 percent of women and 77 percent of men say being an entrepreneur contributes to their happy marriage/ relationship.

Source: OPEN from American Express
Small Business Monitor

Entrepreneur couples = Success & Happiness!

How do you work family into an association of like-thinkers running a company?

I've shed some light on how married couples might make working together a successful enterprise. But how about having other family people working within your business operation? This can be a tricky proposition. You may have brothers or sisters, fathers or mothers, children and people married to your children (this category is called in-laws, sometimes referred to as "out-laws"). You may even have your children's in-laws showing interest. Having family work together has real strengths but very real pitfalls. Let's first walk through how you might open the door to direct family members and those who've married into your family (for simplicity, we'll call all of them "family").

Your first step is to assess the family member's potential qualities and how he or she could fit in; at best this is a slippery slope. There has had to be some expression of interest, at some point in time, between you and your family member. Or it's possible you have observed a specific family member you feel could contribute and grow within your organization. Next, you need to get a feel for that person's desire or motivation; you need to avoid forcing ideas and overselling excitement about how the individual may prosper with you. When you feel there is interest, you can then proceed to showing the person the opportunities he/she may experience by joining you.

Once you have laid out the opportunities and the person wishes to proceed further, it's time to allow a glimpse as to what you would expect from the person and how he/she might help "create and share in the wealth." You will express to the person how you feel his/her strengths may work well within a specific area of your operation. Finally, when you see the person is sold on it, motivated, and vibrating with excitement, it's time to lay it on them: it's an experiment! You're opening a door for the person that may or may not work. It has to evolve into something that works both for the person and for your business. You lay out a program where there will be work evaluations for two consecutive three-month periods. After this period, if it doesn't look good for either the person or the company, it's time to ease the person out.

However, easing out a fallen family member can be an excruciating experience, which is why you need to be very cautious about bringing that person aboard to begin with. A term used by the family patriarch in *Fiddler on the Roof* frequently and appropriately was, "On the other hand." If your family member doesn't work out, you may go through hell to extricate him or her. But on the other hand, if he or she clicks, it's fantastic. You now have shared goals with other family members generating a synergistic excitement. Plus family members will cover your back when problems occur and at crunch time. Generally family members will come together in a crisis and work hard to protect your interests. They know your success and your best interests is also their success and best interests. Besides, if it's your son-in-law, he has to answer to your daughter, right?

Remember our old refrain, "peanuts attract monkeys." If you want to have success, you must pay top dollar to support staff people and offer your production/sales people a percentage of what they bring in. Keeping good people is absolutely critical part to your overall game plan for success now and continued success into your future. This also applies to family members!

We're about to enter the second part of this book, wherein I'll deconstruct some myths that may be keeping you from reaching your fullest potential. To begin, we'll discuss whether it's a myth that one or more college degrees are necessary to strike it big in the business world.

Part Two:

Myths

$ $

Chapter 8

The Education Myth

—————————— $ ——————————

Does a college degree insure success?

The obvious answer is yes, but with a qualifier! All parents would love to see their offspring receive a college degree. Why? It's a distinction achieved by concentration, determination, and organized work. A proud moment for any parents wanting a better life for their child is when that child completes a degree program. It also opens up people's mind to literature, the arts, history—strides made by man from the dawning of the ages to the present. A broader perspective on the world in general and humanity in particular is a must when tasting the delights of the so-called "real world." And of course there is the advantage of having a degree in a desired major, as any employer would prefer getting someone with a degree in the job field versus someone without. Welcome to the real world. But what is the real world? Even with a degree, new graduates may be in for a reality check when they believe they know it all and "the world is their oyster." They don't, and it isn't. You must now deal in the practical application of theory versus actual results.

To achieve success, and I'm talking success rather than happiness right now, a degree gives you a big step forward. (To obtain success plus happiness requires more, which will be covered later.) Along with a degree you must have an inner drive and motivation along with excitement, enthusiasm, and talent. Being excited and motivated comes from enjoying what you do and having the knowledge that your financial remuneration covers your expectations.

But what happens if the degree you receive in your field of choice turns into a job you detest? Or if the companies in your desired field are slow in hiring? Or if the entry level pay is considerably below the standard of living that you were expecting? Or if paying back college loans causes you to frantically find employment that only pays your way versus your being in your chosen field of pursuit? These are questions most college graduates face. However, with a degree you have an important start that bodes well for advancement within any corporate field of endeavor or professional field. This includes even your own entrepreneurial pursuits in contrast to someone without a degree.

Why shouldn't you despair?

Despite the picture painted above, not everyone has been able to get a degree nor had the time, dedication, or financial support to be able to move in that direction. Is all lost if you are one of these people? *No!* Why? Because there are many alternate methods of making success happen. If you are within a corporate organization, big or small, I will outline the means to get ahead. And if you have a bent for the entrepreneurial ideas of starting or picking up your own business, I will present core ideas to you as I go along.

It is extremely important for you to know and understand that many of the most famous people in America had only limited education. Some didn't finish high school while others barely received a high school diploma, yet they found ways to do what before then was thought the impossible. Some of these are well-known success stories such as Thomas Edison at the turn of the twentieth century or Bill Gates of Microsoft at the turn of the twenty 21st century, as of this writing the richest man in the United States. Let's touch on another one of these unique individuals: Henry Ford.

Is a college degree, masters, or doctorate a prerequisite to success?

As we continue to look at the role of education, let's think about Henry Ford, who was more interested in being a "shade tree mechanic" than completing school. Yet he was able to put together a simple vehicle that was low cost and easy to fix—one "you could have any color you want as long as it was black." The tremendous demand for his product brought with it an idea that changed the face of industrialized America: assembly line production where each man did one part of the vehicle as it swung by his station. This revolutionary process multiplied by hundreds the amount of vehicles that could be "rolled out" in comparison to several men working on just one vehicle at a time. Simultaneously the assembly line concept brought the price of the vehicle down to a point that most Americans could afford it.

However, as he grew into fame and fortune, Henry Ford endured considerable criticism. As I understand the story, the press often portrayed him as an ignorant redneck—a blue collar hick who stumbled into the assembly line innovation. One example occurred in 1919 when the *Chicago Tribune* went too far, in effect portraying Mr. Ford as a narrow-minded simpleton who knew nothing of the world beyond his own automobile. Enough was enough: Henry Ford had his team of lawyers file a lawsuit against the newspaper for slander and libel. When the *Tribune* would neither apologize nor retract its comments, the parties went to trial. As the trial progressed, the newspaper's attorneys grilling Mr. Ford did indeed make him seem like the uneducated simpleton they had made him out to be.

Then it was Mr. Ford's lawyers' opportunity to rebut the *Tribune* and present Mr. Ford's testimony. The newspaper's case was shattered when Henry Ford took the stand and was asked about the assertions that impugned his character and his lack of education. "Gentlemen," Mr. Ford testified, "If you came into my office, you would notice a series of buttons. Any question in foreign politics needed answering, I merely press a button. and in comes one of my associates with a PhD in international affairs. Ask me a question on American domestic issues, and in walks another associate with a masters and experience in U.S. governmental affairs. Ask me a question on mechanical engineering, and in walks one of America's premier specialists. Ask me a question on internal medicine and in walks an MD renowned throughout the known world to answer the question. Ask me about current government's economic policy, and in walks a former Fed Reserve official to answer."

Mr. Ford then turned to the jury, who by now were all smiles, and hit them with the coup de grace: **"Members of the jury, I do have my masters and doctorates in any subject you wish—I just press a button, and there they are!"** The jury roared and Henry Ford was awarded the verdict and damages.[2] Uneducated, maybe, but bright absolutely. This story may be an extreme and all the facts may be slightly different than expressed here, but remember: not having a college degree is no deterrent to your achieving the ultimate in success and happiness. There are many other attributes providing you the stepping-stones you'll need. As you read on, I will provide a series of flash points on those specific attributes.

Henry Ford did have his masters and doctorates— press a button and there they'd be!

Why do human genes give us the luck of the draw?

There's been on-going studies on whether it's your gene mix rather than your upbringing that has the most influence on the way you turn out. Approximately fifty years ago, psychologists theorized that 60% of who you are came from environmental conditioning while 40%

---

[2] *Biodun Ajagun, "Who Is an Educated Person?" Saturday Tribune, October 6, 2007, http://www.tribune.com.ng/06102007/opinion.html.*

was due to inherited genes. Studies now indicate these percentages are reversed: at least 60% of how you develop intellectually is based on your genes while 40% or less is based on your upbringing. There's no doubt in this author's mind that 60% to 70% is through inherited genes. How often have you seen someone with a sharp mind hardly break a sweat in school and excel academically while others put in myriad hours burning the midnight oil to achieve similar results? And what about those who just can't quite make it happen irrespective of how hard they work? It's not fair, but it's the luck of the gene draw.

Even within the same family, siblings can differ widely in their abilities to learn and grow their mind. I'm certain if you're gifted with the positive gene draw and it's combined with a good upbringing, you have the best of both worlds working for you. However, the smart genes can only give you the propensity to achieve and grow. Science still does not have a handle on all of the intangibles that allow success to be created. What I do believe is that irrespective of one's IQ, there has to be a sense of urgency driven by a motivation to succeed.

How do you tell a very bright person from a highly educated one?

Bright comes from luck of the positive genes; education comes from motivation to achieve. An argument could be made your luck of the positive gene draw may provide the motivation gene even if your IQ isn't at the top of the chart. We will have to leave this up to the scientists as they research the unknown. So then, who is more likely to succeed—the bright or the educated? Being bright and educated is the ultimate in your pursuit for success. However, if you haven't received a college degree, but you are bright and a quick learner, I will outline some external methods to enhance your opportunities.

Is it possible by alternate means you can learn and earn the equivalency of having a college degree?

Yes, yes, and yes! But how? One of the best ways to earn an equivalency of sorts to a college education is when you directly or indirectly stumble onto a potential career opportunity. An excellent opportunity may allow a motivated person with desire and ambition to pursue certain outlets that allow for escalating growth—growth that allows ascendancy within even an organization populated at the top by those with college degrees.

How do you climb upward and onward when all around you say no? Must you have a degree to have any chance? Part of that answer may be in the following three ways:

$ *Workshops*: There are myriad workshops providing vital information directly applicable to your chosen path. Most will provide you certificates showing your attendance and completion of a specific body of information. These are vital to your growth as they will provide you the latest and best information that puts you in the know. Knowledge is power!

$ SEMINARS: Check out each and every seminar that will give you specific knowledge in your field of choice. You should be able to receive a "Certificate of Completion" that can add to your resume demonstrating you are someone with knowledge and someone to be reckoned with. Stay focused and complete as many of these as you can. Doors will open to you, blue skies will lie ahead, and you'll be flying as high and wide as your enthusiasm and motivation will allow!

$ *Licensing*: Having a license is a must in a number of careers you may want to pursue. Once you get your feet wet and begin to learn your way, the next step is to obtain a license. Almost always having the license opens the door to an opportunity to substantially increase your income. It could be a career in the real estate sales field, the finance industry as a loan originator, or as a stockbroker, now referred to as financial advisor or financial planner. In addition, you may take additional industry studies in the field requiring licensing whereby you obtain designation letters behind your name reflecting the knowledge and experience the designations carry. When specific to a given field, these designations may carry more weight then a general degree. The world becomes your oyster!

And let's not forget the licenses required for various trades. Having expertise with licensing in a variety of technical trades as well as achieving the general contractor's licensing needed in many other fields gives you an opportunity to rise higher and more quickly, thereby increasing your income opportunities. In addition you develop confidence in yourself. The confidence you obtain and the practical experience you develop with your license allows you to partake in the greatest of all things—the American Dream of owning your own successful business.

What provides the greatest potential for success?

I touched on self-confidence. Absolutely, having self-confidence can move mountains. It allows your enthusiasm to be imbued in others with the zeal of a crusader. People listen, pay attention, and become believers in you and your mission! Doors will open to you as never before. Why? Because you have confidence in yourself, and it automatically transfers to others by their having confidence in you.

How about who you might know? Don't miss any opportunity to deal with people you know directly or by having been referred to them. Those you know may know someone who knows someone who is looking for someone just like you. It could be a chance to step up in your career work or a special opportunity to buy into the perfect business, one you have been dreaming of getting into.

A geographic location may be the next best way to find long-term success. Study the demographics of various communities within any given location. Check out the potential for growth in the next ten years. What economic factors are causing the area to grow? Which of these economic factors ties in with the type of career or business move you'd like to make? Remember, one of the most important considerations is an area's growth. Why? For every one person moving into an area, it provides a multiplier of two, meaning every new body in an area creates the need for services employing another two people. Talk about potential for success! If you're merely decent at what you do, your chances are enhanced immeasurably by the numbers of people growing around you.

Does talent provide you an extra dimension for success?

Talent alone does not get it! We all have talent in some area, but how do you determine where your talent lies? Part of it may be trial and error. As you explore various career opportunities, something may evolve where you get "that" feeling. For example, your feeling may come from the ease of doing a certain type of job assigned to you. Where others become bogged down, you find yourself sailing through with effortless energy and positive motivation.

Or perhaps you receive a pat on the back and compliments from others that cultivate internal feelings building confidence. Your excitement level rises and your enthusiasm to accomplish and succeed soars. As this occurs, you will find a talent you never realized was there. Once you feel, understand, and accomplish—and find others are feeding into this positive ability of yours—you will know it. Your talent and confidence then provides the extra dimension needed to propel you to success!

Does IQ guarantee success?

If you believe you have an above-average IQ, *yes*, it absolutely helps you. So many young men and young women have plodded through years of academia, received a BS, BA, or master's degrees, yet lack certain special qualities that lead to true success! You may succeed despite not having an upper-level education simply because a sharp, quick mind is an ingredient along with other attributes pointed out to you here that will propel you to succeed. There are no guarantees. However, with a good mind you can fit all the pieces together that may take you further, wider, and higher than you ever expected.

How about looks?

It is absolutely true, "looks are only skin deep." So let's take a look at some of the myths concerning looks. Yes, looks make a tremendous difference in someone else's perception of you. Experts have written that cute babies get more hugs and more attention and develop greater confidence as they grow up. Remember the teacher's pet? It wasn't the ugly duckling of your class, right? We must take advantage of what God gave us. When you factor looks into the overall equation, they fit neatly into your opportunities for future success in any field or endeavor.

However, do not despair if you feel God hasn't served you well in the looks department. Being well-groomed is a fantastic asset. People enjoy being around someone who looks clean and smells nice. As your author, I'd like to relate something told me as a young man about my grandfather. He was a barber in a small village in the Portuguese island of Terceira in the Azores island chain. In the early part of the twentieth century, there was no radio and no TV. Consequently the village barber shop was where all the confessions, rumors, advice, and counsel were dished out, usually dispensed by the village barber/psychologist.

The story was related to me by my Azorean cousin, who in turn had heard it from his uncle—got it? When I was visiting and checking out my Azorean roots, my cousin said, "Our grandpa, Francisco the barber, constantly heard complaints from his older patrons about how younger people didn't want to be around them. One day he decided to speak his mind by counseling them with these words: "You smell, your clothes smell, your hair smells—who wants to be around you but me?" Such a simple message, but it hit me right between the eyes. He continued, "Wash each day, brush your teeth, comb your hair, clean your clothes, powder yourself, add some perfume, and see what happens." A lesson I have carried with me every day since my visit there in 1973.

Obviously the expression "looks are only skin deep" implies other weaknesses the person may have. I've tried to show you how looks properly used are another great advantage. But so is how a person talks and walks. Much of what we have is through the gene pool of our ancestors. The gift of being able to talk comfortably with eye-to-eye contact is essential in positive communications with each and everyone with whom you come into contact. If you look into the eyes of the littlest of people in the same way as the biggest, you've got the gift.

How you walk is another gift you may have been given. Do you strut or preen? There is an old expression I was taught as a salesperson: "The greatest and most lasting impression a new prospect may have of you is while observing your last few steps before introducing yourself. As you approach a new person you are closely observing them as well as they are absolutely observing you. Your first and most lasting impression is generally made as you walk up to your new prospect. How you walk, how you talk, and how you look overall is a moment captured in time."

Success: Does personality do it?

Another important link to making it whether or not you have a college degree is how you appear to others. Some people have those special personality traits from their gene draw, but most must cultivate them. You've heard the old expression, "Give a nasty look and get one back." The reverse is, "Give 'em a smile and get one back!" You can captivate people with a pleasant, heartwarming smile. Having an upbeat manner is contagious to all you meet. How often have you heard "enthusiasm makes the difference"? Some people come by this naturally—you may be one, but like most people, you may have to work on it.

What role does the mind, heart, and gut play in personal growth?

A balance of these three factors can play an important role in shaping your current thinking and future planning. The mind is your brain's logical thinker; it processes information much like a computer. It gives you the "just the facts, ma'am." Your heart processes information in an emotional manner. It may have you jump on an idea in a flash, then just as quickly create second thoughts. Your gut is believed to be the most intuitive of the three human organs mentioned. It is thought the gut is tapped into a greater or higher power. Unquestionably the reaction to your brain's stimulation coupled with your heart's reaction ignites a feeling in the gut you must not ignore. Deepak Chopra calls it, "the unknowned manifesting itself into the knowned." Pay attention to those gut-level feelings as they will help direct you.

What percentage of college enrollees know what they want to pursue in life?

My personal observation is that less then 25% of college enrollees have a clue as to what major they should pursue. Most college students are in the dark as to the most important decision in their lives. From my experiences and interactions with family and friends, it appears many postgraduate college students are not certain about their major. Consequently most use a hit-and-miss approach and may change their majors many times before getting a degree. Even after they receive a degree and secure a position, doubts often creep in: Did I make the right decision? Will I be happy doing this type of work for my whole life?

Why may college graduates not be prepared?

Having a college degree says a lot about people. It shows they had the persistence to pursue their education through good times and bad, ups and downs, the same as the "real world" of work and career. However, for recent college graduates, the real world of work may be like jumping into a cold shower. There is a shock factor. They must apply their education—which is largely theoretical—to the reality of practical experiences. Their training ground is their new work environment, and they may not like what they've gotten into. But there's always a light ahead.

Why would you benefit from furthering your education?

Almost any corporation large or small, or even small business organizations look first to hiring you based on a college degree. New bosses like it, as they want the feeling of confidence they receive by knowing you have paid the price to get that degree. To them, this means you will be willing to pay the price to make it happen for this new employer by virtue of your work ethic and stick-to-it-iveness. You also benefit by having your employment application placed on top of a to-be-reviewed pile. Consequently you may have more options open to you than someone without a degree. But let's not forget technical school education. Certain businesses look for completion certificates showing skills learned in a particular field.

How can training on the job accelerate your potential to succeed?

As I mentioned earlier, taking advantage of company workshops, training seminars, and courses for special accreditation can help you quickly climb the corporate ladder. Adding in a positive attitude, willingness to accept constructive criticism, and sharing of credit or blame with others will be a plus for you. Making positive contributions and sharing the credit is a surefire way to shoot to the top.

Why do extremely self-directed people hit the wall?

Of course you must also be prepared to be patient and wait for your opportunity to jump ahead. Sometimes you're in a situation where you wait and wait, and either the family members lurking in the wings or the tenure of older employees prevent you from getting what you feel is rightly yours. You feel you're not getting the breaks. You feel time is running out. You feel stuck at a level beneath your ability and income-earning potential. Finally you hit the wall! You know there has got to be better things out there for you. At this point, whether or not you have a college degree, all you have learned to date comes to the forefront.

You are now positioned to check out the opportunities of a true entrepreneur. Your time has come! Remember a college degree is not critical to a lifetime of success. As we discussed earlier in this chapter, you are the sum of your attributes. You now feel a change is imminent, time to start looking for a way out as well as a way in. A college degree may open doors, but ultimately it's who you are and what moves you that counts. Have a positive attitude—it could move mountains. A word of caution, however: do not allow yourself to use a Positive Mental Attitude (PMA) to forge ahead into what may become a negative situation for you. The next chapter on the "Bloody Pulp" Theory will illustrate and make you aware of potential pitfalls. Read on.

Chapter 9
The "Bloody Pulp" Theory
$

What is the "Bloody Pulp" Theory?

Many of you have read and delved into your own attempts at using a Positive Mental Attitude (PMA) to reach your desired goals, correct? Scores of "attitude books" have been and are prevalent in bookstores throughout the United States. A PMA is paramount to your success, but in balancing your attitude and steadfast intractable methods of achieving your goals, you must be aware of what I call the "Bloody Pulp" Theory. Here's some real world experiences with PMA driving home the point:

Reading a book on PMA was an exciting, enlightening, and life-changing experience for me. I went on to read the second, then the third, then the fourth books on the subject—and away I went. I was hooked! Yes, I thought, all I need to do is focus on any goal I want to achieve, have unswerving confidence that it will happen, and *it will happen*!

As there was nothing stopping me, all I had to do was confront and overcome any obstacle in my way, right? Let's picture my obstacle as being a huge wall, higher then high, wider then wide, deeper then deep, between me and my desired goal. I'd been advised that to achieve my goal, I must have unswerving conviction, persistence, and determination. I'd have to go "over the wall." If this didn't work, then I must go around it; if that did not work, I must go under it! Finally, if none of these worked. I must smash or break through the wall. And there my good people is all there is to it—or is it?

I did crash through the wall more than once. Guess what? I became a "Bloody Pulp. Why? First, because I was forcing my way through, and second, because it takes Portuguese people like me a little longer for things to literally sink in, the result being chaos, disorientation, and failure. It came to mind there must be a better way. The lesson: if you can't go under it, over it or around it, and you're forced to break through it, *don't*!

Do this instead: keep probing to the right or to the left of your obstacle as far as you can go. Or take a 180-degree turn and go in the opposite direction. Guess what? Indirectly you will still reach your goal. It may not be exactly what you expected, but you will not crash and burn, and you'll still be whole. A different path will be the best way for you to go, even if you may not think so at the time. Why? We get caught up in our ego and our will, and we believe we have failed by not achieving the goal as planned. Wrong! I want you to be here to live another day. Follow along as we hope to uncover and provide you an armload of pertinent ammunition for your success.

"Bustin' through" is great—but you might become a "Bloody Pulp"!

How can you use life's negative experiences to your benefit?

You must thoroughly and completely evaluate each setback. Within each setback you can determine the misstep and overcome failure by taking corrective action. Take a good look at what didn't work for you and why. Make sure you're not on a "pioneering venture" (more on this later). Another approach is to emulate others having had success in the same field you're exploring. Check with people who have knowledge of others successful in their own efforts. They in turn can direct or refer you to just the right individual who can uncover your failed effort and aid you onto a successful new path.

Why do some fail and remain failures and others learn from failure and succeed?

An ability to regroup and redirect is essential. Evaluate all steps taken in trying to reach your goal, and attempt to uncover the steps you took that created a misfire. Then put together a new plan by redirecting your efforts with the zeal of a crusader. Internal motivation is crucial to jumping back into the fray and giving it another shot. Having a burning desire is a catalyst propelling you forward. Some have this desire, others don't—which one are you? Remember: failures give up, winners don't!

Why does steel dipped in fire become stronger?

A chemical reaction occurs when a piece of steel is placed into a furnace at high temperatures. Tempering steel is the result of heating it to red hot, then having it cool instantly causing an extreme hardening. This also occurs in your mind when a failure creates a negative mental reaction. Trial by fire creates a new resolve to use the hard lessons learned to overcome and succeed. This new resolve can create strength from your new knowledge and experience. In turn you can convert this new knowledge into determination—and acting on this determination can create positive new results.

How can you use less effort to accomplish more?

Does this sound like an oxymoron? This question definitely appears to be a contradiction, so how is it possible? You've had a specific goal, you've set your plan of action in place, and you've charged forward with a newly found energy. You may even move forward with reckless abandon fed by your motivation and belief that a Positive Mental Attitude will carry you to the promised land. But beware!—you may be about to crash and burn. Remember, push hard, then back off. Give it all you have, but if you see trouble ahead in accomplishing your specific goal, *stop*. Let things settle a little, see if somewhere in your desire to nail down that illusive goal other possibilities can open up to you. Is anything happening on the goal end of your effort allowing a positive resolution? If not, rethink and redirect your efforts. It's time to back off and allow the game to come to you. If it doesn't, you need a new game!

How can the ego be the cause of your forcing the issue instead of backing off?

We all have our pride, and in some of us, it could take the form of a giant ego. When you proceed with achieving a goal, and it's a goal you must achieve at all costs, no way can you back away. Why? Your ego can't stand the thought of failure. Still, it must be done. Once the seed is planted in your mind, your ego gets involved, and tells you this is the way and the only way. You're not a quitter; you don't want to lose face. When you make a commitment, people know you're not one to back out. But beware: you don't want to become a "Bloody Pulp" victim. Stop, look, and listen—there will be a better way for you.

Why may forcing and exerting negative energy prevent creative solutions from coming naturally?

Pressure can be negative. Pressure to reach your goal or die trying can eat you up inside and destroy your ability to think rationally. You become desperate; you become anxious; you cannot fail. However, your specific goal now is looking bleak. It's time for you to pause, sit back, think it through, and let it unfold. There is a right plan out there for you. It may not be the way you feel something must be done, but it is there waiting for a solution that may only come when you allow it to open up naturally.

How do you benefit by not blaming yourself or others for negative events?

When you blame yourself for falling short of your goal, negative reactions set in. Negative feelings cause a loss of confidence, which can then cause a retrenchment in projecting your desires. It may cause you to either give up or completely back off. Blaming others is an attitude that you must shake off immediately. Remember, these were *your* goals, not someone else's. Don't blame anyone or anything. Keep your mind clear and uncluttered. By not blaming anyone including yourself, you can unclutter your mind and provide a breeding ground for positive solutions.

How can a severe problem have within it the root source of its solution?

I believe we have to credit author Napoleon Hill in *Think and Grow Rich* with an expression I firmly hold as an absolute truth: "Every negative event has the seed of a bigger & better benefit."[3] This is good stuff! If your experience leads you to believe that your plan is flawed, take time to go through every step of your plan determining what you should or could have done differently. Attempt to uncover where you may have been blocked or otherwise prevented from crossing the final hurdle. Tap into your heightened senses created from the intense pressure to succeed. Brainstorm corrections, as ideas will follow taking you in new directions and to new opportunities allowing you to fly as high and wide as your imagination will allow!

When can taking the line of least resistance be the best way?

Your first thought may be that taking the line of least resistance is synonymous with taking the easy way out. In some cases that may be true; however, when it comes to locking in on a goal, you need

---

[3] *Napoleon Hill. Think and Grow Rich, rev ed. (1937; repr., San Diego: Aventine Press, 2004).*

the latitude we've been discussing. Battle scars from forcing the issue may become abundant; they may even be fatal to the weaker among us. Forcing an outcome because your expectations are too high could cause a failure—or a string of them. It's possible when your rigidly set goals do not materialize that you're prepared to throw up your hands and give it up. What now? Try this: take the pressure off.

Let's use a basketball analogy. You may have heard a TV announcer say, "The new player on this team has been forcing his shots and missing. But now we've noticed he's allowing the game to come to him; he's in the flow of the team. He's achieved a new confidence showing up in his scoring and ball handling." You too can achieve the same result by backing off, taking the line of least resistance, and allowing a natural flow to occur. When it feels right, you'll know it!

Are you forcing your way on others and wondering why your results have been negative?

I'm now addressing how you may be discussing, presenting, and negotiating with people regarding ideas to create working relationships or contractual relations. You've prepared an idea and worked up a presentation. Now you approach the prospect, sit down with the person, and present the deal of a lifetime (or so you may think). You then go for the close. The prospect needs time to think about it. You suggest a certain time the next day for the two of you to talk. But when you call at the appointed time, you're told, "Sorry, he/she's not here." When you ask when the person will be back, you hear, "Don't know." So you leave your phone number with a request for the person to respond, but there's no call back that day or the next morning. So you call again: "Hey, I've been trying to reach you regarding the plan we discussed." The response, "Sorry, I've been busy—I still need time to think about it."

You then ask if you can call tomorrow at 10:00 a.m. The response? "Sorry, I won't be here then. But, hey, I've got your number—let me call you back, okay?" Where do you think you are with this prospect? Getting frustrated? Damned right you are.

So what can you do? First you need to be a good listener and try to understand your interviewee's needs. Then find out what it is the person may have to offer that allows you to soften your position and give him/her more of what they want or need. As you move through the negotiations, you will begin to get a sense of where the interview is going. In that spirit, here's an approach that outlines the manner in which successful negotiations must *always* be approached. This can accomplish crucial goals such as bringing that skeptical person aboard or nailing down the nervous client on a sale or a working relationship.

There has to be a meeting at the middle. What does this mean? Let's draw a mental picture: say you have a fence with a ledge on top between you and your neighbor's house. You're standing on one side with your elbows on the ledge and your prospect is on the other side. As you continue your presentation, you begin to notice your prospect edging away from the fence ledge. Of course you don't want to give up on him. However, if you notice the prospect continue to back away, please *don't* reach over the fence and try to drag him to the ledge in the middle. There has to be a mutual consent. When your prospect reaches up and puts his elbows on your fence ledge, you've got a deal. You must meet halfway, and if you have to reach over the top to bring your prospect to the middle—forget it. It's not going to work now, and it's not going to work in the future.

If they don't meet you half way, "forgeddaboutit"!

When you are unable to reach common ground or come to the middle, resistance begins to build. Resistance causes friction, friction creates heat, heat causes frustration, frustration creates pressure, pressure causes negative reactions, negative reaction creates anger and fear—and both of these are short and long-term deal killers. So where do you go from here? How do you avoid resistance and not lose your opportunity? You don't. Step away, step aside, go for your next prospect, your next, and your next. They are out there. Then all of a sudden you arrive at a day when your new prospect places his/her elbows on your ledge and looks you square in the eye. Thank God, you've got a deal.

Why should you remain open to all the options that may be available rather than locking into one?

Here's an approach I've chosen to use that I offer it to you as a suggestion. Call each new idea and each new plan you wish to implement an experiment. Why? To explain, I must tell you a story. I've operated as an entrepreneur for many years, and as a result I've encountered multitudes of others who were also entrepreneurs. An entrepreneur is generally a highly independent individual. Let me tell you about one who we'll call Charlie. He could never be pinned down to specific results or set percentages when working on a deal. At one point, I became so frustrated with him, I asked, "Why can't we nail down some specifics?" His response was, "No way—no one is going to stick my feet in concrete then shoot me right between the eyes!"

This man drove me crazy! I didn't buy into his convoluted thinking. However, it did allow me to evolve a new approach I could live with. Why not call a new plan an experiment? It takes the heat off. Lay out your plan, lay out your specific conclusions, then make sure all involved know this is what you expect. By calling it an experiment, you are allowing for flexibility, for tweaking, for a change in direction, for modification. The idea of calling a plan an experiment can scare the bejesus out of most people. Their first reaction is to think you are expecting failure. No, you are expecting success, but success that may come from allowing things to evolve.

Remind your nervous entrepreneur that our United States of America is an experiment in progress. There may come a point where your plan may spit and sputter and run out of steam. So okay! It was an experiment, right? Pick up the pieces and develop a new plan. You are *never* defeated when calling a new plan of action an experiment.

How can an experiment take the heat off of those attempting to make a plan work?

Have you ever been around good people with high-minded principals? They believe in right and wrong as being black and white. It's their way or the highway. It's good to be single-minded in your determination to make something work, but when single-mindedness destroys you if you can't do so, it's no good. I'm sure you're quite aware of an old expression, "Bend, don't break." Calling a plan of any kind an experiment prevents you from falling victim to another old adage, "do or die." An experiment allows you flexibility and peace of mind, and if it doesn't work, it allows you to fight the good fight another day.

Can an idea today be premature and ahead of its time, but work later?

It's important to evaluate plans of action in regards to any endeavor. It's amazing how the passing of time and the changing of events can reopen the door to successfully reviving a former failed plan. At certain intervals, check back on past attempts and review aspects of your plan such as where weak spots may have caused your plan to founder. Let's assume a similar idea comes back up and you feel you'd like to take another swing at the plate. Revive the former plan, add in the specifics you feel were initially missing, then play it out. To use clichés to sum it up, go for broke and let the sparks fly, then if the wheels come off, okay, so that was another experiment. But you may also be surprised, as your plan may fly the next time around and you'll be in hog heaven!

How does relinquishing your ego put the world at your doorstep?

Your ego mirrors all the material things society offers. Your having the biggest and best home on the block or a car just a little nicer or more expensive than your neighbor's. Dressing up with the latest designer clothes. Giving yourself a title creating the recognition others crave. Ego is the driving force of your outer surface, making you desire all the material things of the world before all else. But this incredible and insatiable appetite to achieve and have the very best of all things comes with a price. This price may be your spouse, your children, your working associates, and your extended family. What is your most cherished prize in life? Beware when your ego needs control every aspect of your life. Relinquishing your ego and putting others first is the true measure of happiness and fulfillment. We'll have more on this subject in later chapters.

How can doing less create more?

This is a tough concept to get your mind around. It's based on logical reasoning that at first appears illogical: pushing hard and backing off. You want a certain goal to be fulfilled; you want it so bad you can taste it. Your conscious mind is drumming into you day and night. You must succeed, you have to succeed, and it's driving you crazy! Again, back off, and plug this into your subconscious mind: "I know what I want, and I will merely look over my goal and try to remain detached from the results." There will be more on detaching later. Forcing issues may create scattered results. Beware of losing focus on exactly what it is you wish to achieve. By remembering to "plug it in, then let it flow," you will ultimately accomplish what is best for you. It may not be exactly as you thought it should be; however, it will happen.

In summary, remember to always, *always* set goals. Without goals, your subconscious mind can provide your conscious mind only with bits and pieces of scattered thoughts. It's important to organize these thoughts into goals that in turn give your life a focus. You must be positive in your total resolve. It's vital for you to have tremendous motivation and enthusiasm about how to accomplish your dreams. As you move forward, take pressure off of yourself by letting events flow. Remember! Temper your zeal with the knowledge your inner calm is working for you, and it will happen.

So go for it, but then back off and let it flow. By doing so you may prevent our "Bloody Pulp" syndrome from occurring. As new ways are discovered and open up for you, your mental attitude will begin to soar. You are now onto your next step in this exciting life's journey. As these lessons continue, keep in mind a Positive Mental Attitude can work for you, but it can also work against you. Read on.

Chapter 10
Positive Mental Attitude Myth
―――――――――― $ ――――――――――

Why can PMA cause the "Bloody Pulp Syndrome"?

A Positive Mental Attitude is much like a loaded weapon: You'd better know how to use it or it can kill. Forcing a goal issue is like using your handgun with your gun's safety off—you never know when it will accidentally explode and eliminate the very thing you want. As I have said over and over again, being afraid of failing is one of those triggering mechanisms that cause you to never know when to quit. You must not allow your PMA conditioning to prevent you from understanding when you've reached the point of no return. "Never saying never" by using a PMA to provide focus for an ultimate worthwhile goal is excellent and necessary. However, if you can't go over it, under it, or around it, beware of trying to ram through it— if you do, you will become a "Bloody Pulp."

Why do experts pushing a Positive Mental Attitude create a bogus solution for you?

The belief in a PMA being the end all to reaching goals was first preached heavily in the 1960s. It's continued into the twenty-first century. Why? Because it does work. No question about it—you must be relentless in your pursuit of achieving success. What is being advocated here is to use a small dose of common sense. Your competitive desire, your desire to not fail at any cost, may have the seed within it of your potential failure. I don't mean you should procrastinate or evaluate to a point where you see a bogeyman behind every tree; just don't use reckless abandon as a miraculous crutch. Failure to achieve a goal may cause irretrievable damage to your psyche. It's amazing how a small success here and a small success there can catapult you to greatness whereas a failure can stick in your craw for some time and may even prevent some people from trying again.

How can you maintain your confidence?

One of the biggest obstacles to your success is a loss of confidence. Losing your confidence goes along with a loss of self-esteem, and it can be a killer. Is there a way to avoid this happening? There's an old saying, "Once burnt, twice shy" that means overcoming a loss of confidence is not easy. It requires reaching down deep into the gut, analyzing exactly what may have cost you reaching your special goal, then sucking it up and creating a new plan—a plan that causes your adrenalin to flow with anticipation and new desire. Make a note of this other old saying that makes sense, "Bend, don't break." Keep this in mind as you use the almighty PMA to propel you to success. You have a straight path ahead, a direct route to your heart's desire. But you must be prepared to make the twists and turns and avoid the pitfalls. You can always expect the unexpected. In doing so you must learn to back off, take another look at the situation, and find a way to either improvise or abandon your goal. Knowing there will always be a new day helps keep up your confidence level.

What causes a person to fail?

There are many reasons a person fails. One in particular is laying out goals that are unreachable. Mentors of salespeople will often say, "Set your goal a little bit higher than you feel you can accomplish, but not so high you may never reach it!" You must not allow yourself to become a victim of overzealously shooting for the moon. When a goal is set too high and you fail to reach it, it's like a kick in the stomach.

It can take all the steam out of you so you feel your failure. Instead, ease into setting your goals a notch higher each time, then as you reach and achieve your next plateau, guess what? You feel a sense of accomplishment. Continue to reset your next goal higher. By doing it in achievable increments, you'll take each step of the way with greater enthusiasm and with soaring self-confidence!

Another concern is perceived competition. People get too hung up on what others in the same industry are accomplishing to the point they may feel panic and uncertainty if they aren't matching them. This causes many to crash and burn as they aren't able to take the heat. In prior and future chapters, you will receive more regarding competition and who your *real* competition is.

How does failure affect your psyche?

Failure creates fear, fear causes procrastination, and procrastination creates immobility. You become stagnant in your ability to think creatively as your mind is in a locked position. You are constantly looking back at the problems and reasons that led to your dramatic failure. Looking back instead of forward is fine if you are attempting to find solutions to your missteps, but there's no way it can help if you become mentally mired down with constant negative thoughts. I'm sure you've heard of the reverse of PMA— NMA, or a Negative Mental Attitude. Once a person becomes so immersed in NMA it's akin to a pilot trying to pull out of a nosedive. If you allow yourself to be engulfed only by a sense of failure, there's no pulling out—and you will crash and burn.

How does failure affect our confidence?

A serious failure has a tremendous impact on your confidence. Once you experience a loss in confidence, it spreads throughout your entire being, creating a mental paralysis. You become unsure of every new step you take. Uncertainty puts you into a state of haphazard and fragmented thinking. It can also create a feeling like being frozen stiff—you can't think; you can't act; you can't move in any direction. Inhibitions set in that in turn cause turmoil affecting your whole life.

Why does failure affect your relationships?

You don't have to be a rocket scientist to know how failure can directly affect your personal life. Your spouse may begin to question your ability and begin losing faith in you. Next you may find your marriage on the rocks. If your spouse, your best friend, starts to doubt you, how on a short-term basis do you overcome it? And how about your friends—do you expect them to hang on with you until the bitter end? How do you feel when the office secretary says, "He's not in!" and calls to the person's home are not returned? When the only calls you receive are from your creditors? Friends become scarce to nonexistent, and the doubters abound. Are there solutions?

Can any experts provide easy answers?

One of many ways to begin to rebuild your weakened psyche is to dive into books pushing motivational materials. It's true you might run into what I call "rah rah authors"—the ones looking through rose-colored lenses and seeing only positive solutions to anything and everything. However, most authors paint a more realistic picture of what you should do. Learn from them. Books can give you new and refreshing insight into changes you can make in attitude and goal setting that in turn can lift your confidence from a feeling of failure to exciting new heights of euphoria. Remember, a big reason for your despair could have been your setting unrealistic goals in the first place.

What can we learn from past experience?

Let's repeat the wonderful old saying, "once burnt, twice shy." Heed this advice as it may keep you out of harm's way. Try to study every aspect of your attempt at reaching your failed goal. Pick apart every step, and analyze the steps you should have and will stay away from on your next go around. As you educate yourself through your process of trial and error, a clearer picture will emerge—one having seeds of potential success rather then potential failure. Another method helping you learn from your prior missteps is to learn from others. Whatever goal you strived for has been tried by others. Study carefully the methods used by those that led to success and compare what you tried with their efforts. What worked for them?

How can failure be turned to success?

One of the best ways you may recover from the slings and arrows of failure is to jump back into the fray. Evaluate each detail as you work your way through your failed plan. It bears repeating: you must evaluate in as an objective way as possible. The clichés "stop, look, and listen" and "keep your ear to the ground" do have meaning.

But once you have covered every angle, don't start procrastinating. It's time to redirect and grow! Set up new and exciting goals with a positive direction—goals you feel have been refined and honed for accomplishment. You will then feel your whole being filled with a sense of excitement and euphoria, and this inspiration can take you as high, far, and wide as you wish to go.

When can failure be good?

Your first answer is probably n-e-v-e-r! However, this material does point out situation after situation from which you can learn and become thoroughly educated as to miscues you may be able to redirect. Acknowledging the mistakes leading to failure is not a sign of weakness, it's a sign of *strength*. Another old saying is, "If you understand a problem, it's half solved," so by carefully examining and taking apart the reasons behind a failed effort, you will be way down the road to realistic methods of solving the other half. Reassess and put together a modified plan, and after you retool and reset, *go* for it!

How many failures can we overcome in life?

All but your last failure! You certainly don't want to put yourself in a position of a failure at the end of your productive and active years. If you reach for a speculative goal with no years left to correct and it fails, then all you can do is rationalize your position and hang on to your health. Have your life's relationships in balance and put your best foot forward. However, otherwise, whether you're in your early years or middle years of working and setting goals, a current failure in reaching your specific goal is no reason to withdraw. Snap out of it by taking time to study the successful people who plotted the same goals and succeeded. Emulate their methods and use the tips provided you in prior paragraphs, then march forth with a positive resolve to overcome any failure.

How can calling failures an experiment help you psychologically to redirect?

Life lessons learned can be a blessing. It's important psychologically to trick yourself by always calling a goal for a new plan an experiment. Why? I'd like to repeat a story from an earlier chapter to emphasize my point. Remember the old-timer who said to me, "No SOB is going to put my feet in concrete and shoot me between the eyes!" Translation: "I don't want to have a specific and guaranteed amount of anything in any agreement. Because if I can't meet my goal, I'll be on the *short end of the stick.* Essentially I would have failed." While a no guarantee on achieving a specific goal took the old guy off the hook, it didn't exactly instill great confidence in his business partners.

Instead, it is highly recommended you call any new plan of action (goal) an experiment. And yes, be specific—let everyone involved know how you and they can all benefit. You then give it your best shot, but in case of a downside, you and your associates knew going in that it was just an experiment on which you might have to fold your tent. If you do, it being an experiment takes the sting out of a setback. Is this a negative way to go about it? Some of you may think so, but let me, someone who has been a "Bloody Pulp," tell you this: calling it an experiment *works*!

How do you win from failure?

Evaluating why a failure occurred may be an enlightening experience. How? You may find a means of redirecting and projecting your goal into an exciting new angle, a direction that may sidestep previous hurdles dooming your venture. Flexibility is another key to bouncing back with a new plan. "Bend, do not break" is an attitude found in men or women achieving their goals with the thought, "Let me fly as high and wide with the sky as my limit." If it didn't work, what next? Redefine or pull the plug. Don't beat your head against a stone wall—remember the pitfalls of the "Bloody Pulp" Theory. By redefining your position and taking another go at it, you may just bring the results of your dreams. Each attempted failure with the appropriate tinkering may bring you closer to a resounding *success*!

Why is necessity the mother of invention?

When you are down and out with few or no options available, it's amazing how your mind can invent ways to cope. It's absolutely incredible how when you have your back to the wall, survival instincts take over. You find your way back to the basics (e.g., food and shelter). Your inner turmoil and anxiety force you to use whatever's at hand to find a way back. Your instincts force you to hold tight and get your bearings. Once the reeling effect allows you to think clearly, you can get back to ground zero. How and what do you do now? First you must tighten your nut; that is, the cost of your housing, vehicles, and any luxuries you previously enjoyed have to be eliminated or downgraded to a life-sustaining level. You are now in a survival mode. Next you must completely redo and retool your goals. First, how do you put bread on the table? Next, what steps must you take to find a way back out of your economic dilemma? Consider streamlining or scrapping your former goals.

How do you pick yourself up and create the energy necessary for an exciting comeback?

It's quite possible you *must* dump your prior goals altogether! Clean your slate! Take a good hard look at what you've done in your recent past—what worked for you? As you analyze and learn from your past, project ideas reshaping your goals enabling you to renew and re-energize so you can move progressively forward. By using what you've learned and analyzing pros and cons, you may be able to reconstruct a plan. Remember: learn about what worked for others in similar situations. Determine how you can use your strengths as you proceed in building a plan step by step. Take it steady. Don't take hasty actions. As you construct a positive new plan, review it every morning and every evening before bedtime. This puts your plan into your subconscious mind, which is always, I repeat, always working for you. More exciting and positive ideas regarding the subconscious will be coming in the following chapters.

Part Three:

$

Magic

$

Chapter 11
The Magic Power of Sharing
—————————— $ ——————————

Biblical teaching: Art or science?

Your author is like many people in the United States who were brought up in a strict religious setting, then found our own beliefs as life is lived and learned. Consequently I don't adhere to any particular teaching by established religions. However, I do believe all major religious teachings are very important. We're on this little ball being jettisoned around the sun as our sun doggedly revolves around its universe. So it's no wonder people have always wanted to know what's it all about. Religions have been formed throughout our planet by human beings needing to understand how they should live, what happens afterwards, and what code of ethics and morals should be established for them and their children to live by.

I do believe there is a universal power that guides all living things. This earth and universe can't be just a freak accident. But we'll touch on some of this later. To repeat an earlier quote from Napoleon Hill, "What you share will multiply, and what you withhold shall diminish."[4] There is no question this is an immutable law of nature.

———————————————————

[4] *Napoleon Hill. Think and Grow Rich, rev ed. (1937; repr., San Diego: Aventine Press, 2004).*

Some may call this law an art or an overused religious expression, but I believe it must be a science. Why? One of several definitions of a science is, "The domain of knowledge obtained by the systematic study of nature."

Human beings are part of nature; consequently we innately understand the benefits of giving and sharing. Consider simple things such as watering a fruit tree and seeing a plentiful crop result, giving a smile and receiving one in return, or sharing your love with your family and getting back true love. So even if you don't believe "sharing will multiply" and "withholding will diminish," you still might give this philosophy of life and business a chance, it does *work*! You want it to work for you, right? Then try sharing the wealth with your associates and see what happens. Or if you remain cynical and feel sharing is for wimps, guess what? You will get back in direct proportion to what you withhold—personnel turnover, unhappy associates, and diminished profits.

What's the best way to help yourself?

I'd like to serve up an analogy as an illustration. Let's say you were a passenger on a luxury liner and it began to sink. You are very fortunate as you get thrown clear of your sinking ship. However, you have no life preserver, and all about you are screaming for help. How do you save someone if you're drowning? First, you try to find a life preserver, then you try swimming to a lifeboat. Only then if successful can you begin to reach out to help and save others.

There's no difference in business. First you need to make sure you have you own lifeline, getting your business moving forward before you can reach out. Once you provide a little stability and you're ready to grow, it's time to set up a long-term plan. Within your plan you are determining how to provide a successful path for yourself. What is it? It's back to a basic philosophy of *sharing*, knowing if you want to succeed, you must help others within your organization to succeed. As they succeed the law of sharing kicks in and helps guarantee your success!

How can one share if the other doesn't?

Remember when you were a kid and your mom made a tasty hot apple pie? You'd steal into her kitchen and beg for a great big piece before dinner. As you were her favorite, she'd say, "I'll give you a bigger piece now if you promise to allow your brother, sister, and dad to share the rest of the pie at dinner." Your answer was, "Yes, Mom, absolutely." Now dinner is almost over and it's time for you to allow your family to share the rest of it. But no, you loved that pie, and you insist on sharing in it too. Your mother admonishes you about your promise, but you don't care—you want more. And you get more even though it leaves your family disgruntled, upset, and discombobulated, but you don't care.

When building an organization by extending your philosophy of sharing, you would think your recipients of this largesse would pass it on to the new associates they bring in whereby they could obtain a piece of their new person's future production. One would think a current associate who came aboard with you because he or she loved your philosophy would recognize any new person given a like commission plus bonus sharing plan would also prosper and grow. However, ironically, this is not necessarily true. It always amazes me how some management associates don't get why the sharing concept works. Quite often current associates when faced with having to share their piece of a bonus action with someone new will say no way! They don't understand by sharing and providing incentives, their recruited associates will have greater motivation to do more. They just don't get it. Some don't understand by keeping more of the pie for themselves, they may gain at first, but in the long haul they lose. They become subject to the turnstile effect, constantly training new people and having unhappy, unmotivated, and unproductive people. Fortunately most of our associates, especially the ones who stick with us, do understand.

Is it a natural thing to be greedy?

In the 1985 movie *Wall Street* there was a scene where Gordon Gekko (played by Michael Douglas) needed to explain his motives for a large company takeover to worried corporate stockholders and angry company executives. These executives one by one had essentially called him greedy, dishonest, destroyer of companies, and even un-American. He in turn chastised the hundreds of VPs all earning over two hundred thousand dollars annually, who were enjoying their jet planes, yachts, special vacation homes, and foreign travel despite their company losing one hundred million dollars. He claimed to have researched what it was they did for the company, but that no one could figure it out. This got a positive buzz from the shareholders.

He then got into the meat of his impromptu speech, blowing everyone away when he said, "Greed is good! I am not a destroyer of this company; I'm a liberator of it. Greed is good. Greed works. Greed is right. Greed clarifies, cuts through, and captures the essence of all evolutionary spirit. Greed in all its forms (greed for life, money, love, knowledge, etc.) has marked the upward surge of mankind. And greed, mark my words, will not only save this company but the malfunctioning corporation called the USA!"[5] Stockholders let out a cheer that rattled the rafters! I certainly buy his concept, and I'd like to coin it as "greed for good." However, is it natural to be greedy? Maybe so, as a human being does have natural tendencies for survival, and even misplaced and misunderstood tendencies in everyday life. So are we endowed with certain feelings based on our nature?

Human beings are born with the ability to rationally and logically assess their own actions. But somehow we become muddled about understanding things that should be self-evident. As an example, the story about the bullfrog and scorpion may shed some light:

A bullfrog was crouched alongside a small but swift stream when a scorpion came up to it. The bullfrog warily backed away.

"Don't be afraid," said the scorpion, "I just need to ask you a favor. I need to get to the other side of the stream, so could I get on your back as you swim across?"

"You must be crazy," replied the bullfrog, "You could sting me on the way across and that would be the end of me."

"No, no," said the scorpion, "If I were to sting you and you went down, I'd drown too."

The bullfrog thought a moment, figured the scorpion made sense, and said, "Jump on—let's go." Halfway across the stream, the scorpion stung the bullfrog.

As the bullfrog began to sink and drown, he gurgled, "Why did you sting me?"

---

[5] *"Greed Is Good," Wall Street, DVD, directed by Oliver Stone (1987: New York: CBS/Fox Home Video, 2000).*

With his last words, the scorpion said, "It's in my nature!"

So we must be aware of other people's natures so we can both protect ourselves and use their greed for good.

Why does our nature sometimes prevent sharing?

Wanting more can be a motivating force, but it can also cause our demise. It seems to be a natural instinct for us to want all we can get, and when we get it, to want even more. I once worked with a firm that had a highly intelligent and creative leader. He built a financial empire overnight by bringing together a group of associates who were top-notch professionals in certain areas of finance and investment, including pension consultants, limited partnership attorneys, CPAs, insurance and financial planners, stockbrokers, and business consultants. He was an entrepreneur and creative force. We all loved his approach to building a bigger pie in which we could all share. However, there was one slight problem: he couldn't make good use of his time. By having to make final decisions on each associate's clients, he cut off our ability to do what we'd already mentioned—follow up and follow through. Meetings that dragged on for hours with clients stewing in waiting rooms caused a downward spiral eroding the credibility of all company associates and mostly of our leader. He had great instincts in bringing top people together, but his need to hoard his control destroyed what he created.

You as a start-up business owner and entrepreneur must use your natural instincts when getting your operation off the ground. As you balance the need for top associates, also balance out their responsibilities. While determining how to distribute income to new key people, you must keep in mind how to use your time and energize your people to greater heights. They need a certain amount of freedom to innovate and put ideas into action without every move being watched and critiqued by Big Brother. By putting your trust into your associates, a karmic effect takes place. If you share your trust in them, it will be returned to you many times over. Allowing them to share in control over what they do as well as in profits may not be a natural instinct, but it must be one you work on constantly to build and keep a highly exciting and successful enterprise.

How can one be assured of a flow of riches?

Building an organization with first-class associates is paramount to your company's longevity. These are associates who have come aboard by buying into your personal and business philosophy and who are **excited about pushing your business ideas to both producers and managers.** I see them as the management associates who have the knowledge and moxie to maintain top associates and past clients and still continue to build your company. How can you accomplish this? It has to be more then luck, as it requires planning. Let's assume you have gotten your company past its initial start-up period. Now it's time to put together a permanent plan of the way you will commit to your people as to the way they can share in your company's growth. How you share with them to maintain and develop top associates depends on your unique type of business. It's much easier when you share in a sales type organization by creating extra wealth for your people based on an extra piece of their production pie. Other types of companies may require more intricate production methods whereby associates may share in company wealth they've helped create.

A pitfall one needs to sidestep is having associates appearing to welcome your philosophy upon coming aboard, but after a time you discover they may talk a good game but have quite a different perspective. They love to receive—but down deep hate to give! How do you handle this situation, especially if your associate has been a good individual producer and earner for your company? You are in it for a very long haul as eventually associates who are not like-thinkers will create negative waves. I believe you understand the old expression, "A bad apple spoils the barrel." These people must be eased out, In turn continue to reach out and attract like thinkers, associates who are sincere, hard-working, creative (in other words, a joy to have in your circle), as they will grow and prosper with you. They in turn ensure continued positive growth for years to come. This is as close a guarantee you can have to continued sharing in a flow of riches. This gives you and associates an exciting way to strive, thrive, and survive for many years to come.

How can making others wealthy around you also create wealth for you and your family?

This concept may come across as foreign when you first hear it; however, small and large entrepreneurs have discovered it works. In my case, I saw it happen firsthand. I noticed as we tried taking baby steps to get our new start-up company off and running, several of our new associates were able to create enough success for themselves to purchase new homes. Although I was struggling to juggle cash flow to keep our operation alive, I was happy to see that many of my associates not only raised their own standard of living, but were also able to place their children in private schools and offer their families the finer things in life. It took time but as we continued to "Duplicate Ourselves" with first-class associates and created a larger and larger sales force, their override income began to produce terrific net profits for our company. Technology helped us to keep our support staff and overhead costs down while our gross income rose exponentially. The beauty of this was that as wealth was created, we were able to share it with our associates. Sharing creates wealth for all!

This concept is important as to how you set up your company system. You need to allow associates to come aboard with sufficient opportunities available to them so they can grow as far, as wide, and as high as their desire and motivation allows. To maintain and build a great group of associates, you must give them enough reason to stay with you. Many motivated associates are just like you: they will want to build their own company and grow and expand as they see fit. However, if you build a program where associates can grow from personal production to branch management and then to regional management, you're allowing them to be a circle within your circle. They can add associates, get a percent of your production pie, and still have a support group backing up their hand. Essentially they don't have to reinvent the wheel.

How has hi-tech helped create horizontal management systems?

Corporations are learning that vertical management from the top down creates inefficiencies. In contrast, an interlocking Web system linking all of your top management to your field associates and everyone in between works perfectly as a horizontal management system. It allows instant feedback from corporate support to producers and back again. It ties in with associates having their own independence but still having an opportunity to be interdependent within your successful operation. Your associates as independent contractors in your employ can help create new wealth where you as a company hub can share and grow and experience explosive growth with your motivated associates.

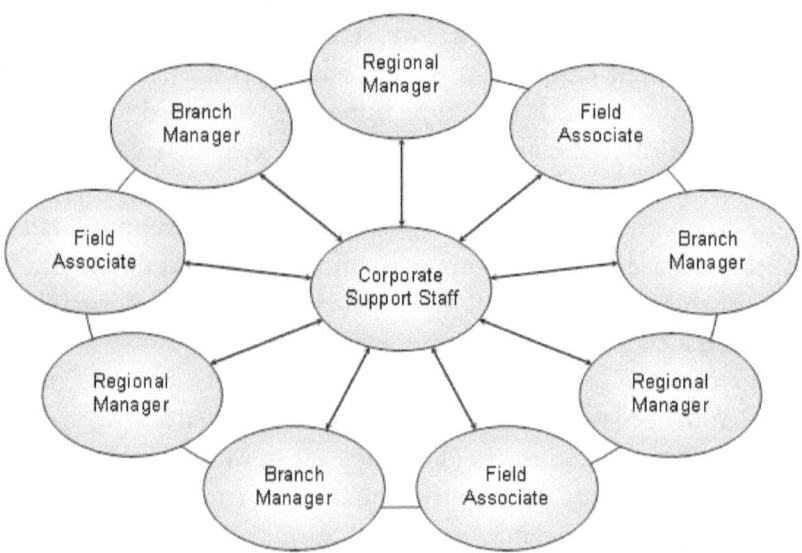

A 21st Century interlocking management web for success!

Using your computer to link you at corporate, with your regional managers, your branch managers and field associates allows a horizontal management style befitting the twenty-first century. Your corporate support staff is linked directly to all of your management teams and field associates—and they are linked directly to you. You're now able to have instant "in out" and "out in" communication directly with all those in your linked Web, whereas a vertical management style involves layers of management bureaucracy that can stifle quick communications. In a vertical management system, there's a president, vice presidents, supervisors, regional managers, branch managers, and field associates run by top-down management, with each having to answer to the one next above. A field agent in a vertical system may never be able to deal directly with top management, thus stifling quick action on potential problems needing a quick fix, etc. Our horizontal management system shows an interlocking Web allowing quick action among all parties and forging a lasting *Interlocking Network Web of Success*. You can take advantage of every hi-tech innovation currently at your disposal and achieve quick and direct communications with an interlocking network of associates creating and sharing wealth.

What besides money can be shared with others?

Remember: your business and your associates are interlocked with you, comparable to the officers and crew of a luxury liner. I must repeat the story about the two ships' captains who had different philosophies on how to conduct their ship's cruises. One believed his officers and passengers would of course be privy to every detail of his ship's voyage; however, he didn't believe it was necessary for his crew to be bothered. The other captain believed his officers, passengers, and crew should be included in every aspect relating to their destination. Which one of these captains had the best ship's morale? If you were part of a ship's crew working down deep in a greasy, noisy, dark engine room, literally kept in the dark, which captain's philosophy do you think would press your hot button?

So too does it behoove you as a business owner to make sure to share every detail of your company's destination. This means letting every level of your personnel understand where you expect to be in six months, in a year, in five years! This way even your lowly backroom copy boy has the feeling he's contributing to your company's success. All of your people—management, sales, and support staff— need to see your vision and enjoy participating and being part of a dynamic team. You can't just treat people like growing mushrooms, 'keeping them in the dark and feeding them horse manure'. Each person in your organization is an integral part of your company's success. 'Top to bottom' and 'out to in and in to out', let them all know where you're going and what they are doing to help, then watch their attitude skyrocket. It's phenomenal.

Besides providing your associates with a vision and goals pointing toward future success, being a patient mentor to them is vital—and it works. There's nothing like a successful business person as a teacher.

Associates with positive attitudes want to learn and grow, so who better to guide and instruct them than you? By sharing your time through office meetings, workshops, luncheon meetings, and spur-of-the-moment "roll up your shirtsleeves" meetings, associates can gain so much more than merely learning by trial and error. Bring them into certain meetings when negotiating for new associates or putting out fires in crisis management meetings, or even company planning meetings. You as a successful business person will be imparting invaluable knowledge on how to run an organization. A gift of your time creates a special synergy with your people catapulting your organization to incredible success.

How do doors open when everything is shared freely?

As mentioned previously, in 1983 I started a mortgage company. It was an experiment, but as my little experiment gained legs, a number of observers and advisors suggested I should create a franchise organization to protect our basic business concept and use it to expand our company with potentially more control. In addition, doing so would protect us from the competition stealing our successful ideas. I decided to spend time and energy studying franchising ideas, then I looked into the legal costs, which were jolting. Next I considered how a franchise model could be set up with a tight organizational management team. The more I delved into it, the more pressure and doubts crept in. Consequently we decided to take the line of least resistance and continue building as we had been doing and see if our "What you share will multiply" philosophy would continue to work.

Over years of evolutionary growth, we determined we could build by keeping a low overhead management style and give back to our associates, in turn preaching our low overhead approach to all our associates who wanted to grow within our operational structure. At first our low overhead approach was used out of necessity; however, as we continued to build, we realized it worked. Keeping overhead down and giving back more of our company's potential profits allowed word-of-mouth referrals—they're the best! In time we noticed the associates who believed and accepted our company philosophy stayed with us and grew by sharing and giving back to the new associates they recruited. The notion of a wheel within a wheel within a wheel is similar to our Interlocking Horizontal Management System. We've shown that independence and interdependence can work hand in hand.

This approach to company growth is analogous to how America's two political parties differ in taxation. One party feels a strong federal government can be more effective if it receives tax revenue in larger abundance, which it in turn can redistribute back in a democratic fashion to meet the needs of our American people. The other party feels keeping taxes lower (or cutting taxes) allows more money to be in the hands of business owners and especially consumers, which in turn allows greater production and income to businesses, thus providing more jobs and greater tax revenues to the federal government. Ultimately this approach allows more money to be redistributed back to social needs, etc. within our country. As a company we prefer to avoid aligning with one political party over another; however, allowing more money to stay with consumers and businesses seems to coincide with our business model of "keeping overhead costs down" and "sharing in created wealth." The more you have to share, the more it will multiply.

Can we give away more than we receive?

I'm sure you've heard this question before. It does seem incongruous if you're advised you can give away more than you receive in return. This needs to be explained in a more logical manner. There's a story about the little restaurant that was selling a luncheon steak sandwich. Everyone in town lined up to buy one. So everyone knew this little but mighty restaurant was earning a fortune, right? Wrong—they were losing twenty-five cents on every sandwich they sold and going broke. True story! Obviously this restaurant business was not on purpose giving away more than it expected to receive. What's the point of this story? You must be positioned to give, but instead of sharing profits before you have profits, you may have to give in time, energy, and teaching. Then you can be in a position to "create the wealth and share the wealth."

How can you lift your own spirits by giving a little something?

Deepak Chopra has noted that while giving and receiving are important in our daily interactions, the purpose you have for doing so will ultimately decide how much you will benefit from these acts. I do believe him; however, it's also important to take a practical view. What's wrong with knowing you are giving because you have expectations of receiving? Let's follow a rationale where you set up a business model "sharing the wealth" because you recognize it brings good people to you—you benefit them and they in turn benefit you. (Sorry, Deepak, I do believe in your teachings, but in this case I'm putting a Western cultural spin to them, okay?)

Chopra's principle of giving is apropos when you consider that as he states, money is really a reflection of and symbol for our life energy. It is the payment for our hard work, and it provides nearly everything with which we sustain ourselves. Money, like life energy, is meant to circulate. Our financial economy thrives by the constant transfer of currency. Our emotional health also improves when we permit positive things to flow from ourselves to others around us. And what we seek from others can only be had if we first give it ourselves.

Deepak Chopra illustrates the magic power of sharing more poetically and in greater depth than I can; I hope you will take the time to seek out some of his writings. Our lessons aren't complete yet. In the next chapter, you will discover how to tap into a special universal power placing you in a position to truly become what you wish. Now let's move on to the magic power of the universe!

Chapter 12

Universal Power

―――――――― $ ――――――――

BEING A SUCCESSFUL ENTREPRENEUR requires more than business smarts or ambition and motivation to succeed—it requires an intangible I call a universal power. Being able to tap into this special power or energy is absolutely critical to achieving success without breaking down physically or mentally.

Why is it possible for an unseen power to work?

As human beings, we pretty much think along the old line of, "Hey, I'm from Missouri. I don't believe it—show me!" Think about this: we live on this small ball spinning around its own axis, rotating around our sun, which rotates around our galaxy, which in turn pinwheels around our universe. Another unseen energy field we call gravity allows us to cling to our little ball. And yet we give hardly a thought about the existence of these unseen things. Let's blow your mind with specifics:

$ **Our Earth is rotating on its own axis at a speed of 1,040 miles per hour.**[6]

―――――――――――

[6] *"How Fast Is the Earth Moving?" Enchanted Learnings, http://www. enchantedlearning.com/subjects/astronomy/planets/earth/Speeds.shtml.*

141

$ **The Earth is also hurtling around our Sun at 67,000 miles per hour.**[7]

$ **Simultaneously our Sun is zooming around our galaxy at 486,000 miles per hour.**[8]

$ **Our Milky Way galaxy is silently and incredibly pin wheeling through space at approximately 600 kilometers per second (51.81 million kilometers per day), at the same time pin wheeling around other galaxies.**[9]

But does anyone other then scientists give this a second thought? No! It's considered to be a phenomenon accepted by a majority of our world's population. But talk about an energy field called our *subconscious mind*, which is part of a *universal power*, and most people will give you a blank look (or worse, think you are slightly unhinged).

Do you know how your heart beats?

Very in-depth scientific information is available complete with all the jargon to intricately explain when a heart starts to beat about twenty-two days after gestation. Again something miraculous is taken for granted. As far as is known, no one has discovered kinetic power (something's ability to run on its own indefinitely). So explain to me in simple terms how your heart starts, and how it continues to beat on its own?

Scientists tell us there is an electric and magnetic field around our Earth that interacts with the sun, with the sun interacting with a constantly moving galaxy. As far as I know, everything that becomes electricity is created by man through one form or another of solar, water (hydraulic), or wind power. So to use electricity to run things, you must

[7] *Amelie Saintonge, "At What Speed Does the Earth Move Around the Sun?" Ask an Astronomer, http://curious.astro.cornell.edu/question.php?number=356.*

[8] *Paul Recer, "Radio astronomers Measure Sun's Orbit Around Milky Way," Houston Chronicle, June 1, 1999, http://www.chron.com/content/interactive/space/astronomy/news/1999/ds/990602.html.*

[9] *Patricia Kong and Glenn Elert, "Speed of the Milky Way in Space," The Physics Factbook, http://hypertextbook.com/facts/1999/PatriciaKong.shtml.*

have a method to plug the thing in somewhere. Is there a "plug in" for your heart? I wonder again how our hearts start beating and what keeps them going? People take for granted this miraculous use of electricity with no concept as to how it's created or how it really works. Most people haven't a concern in the world; it's just another phenomenon taken for granted. But mention an ability for our subconscious mind to somehow connect with an electric energy source (let's call it a universal power or energy), and people begin to freak out.

How do these miracles work?

Man has always tried to understand how our universe began, logically assuming that if something begins, it must end. Many theories and counter theories try to explain it. As science began to get beyond the reach of oppressive religious suppression, theories continued to evolve. Guess what? Most remain just theories, or in other words, a lot of guesswork is involved. I suspect a battle will continue to wage indefinitely between traditional religious thinking and scientific research. So it's no wonder our conscious mind may not comprehend our ability to tap into a universal power, let alone believe it's possible. But is there a universal power that allows our conscious mind to tap into our subconscious mind that is tied into a universal energy or power? I believe there is!

So is there a universal power?

At some point in man's history, we began to wonder if there was something beyond birth and death, ashes to ashes—or is that all there is? Why were we put here to think, procreate, then die if there is nothing else? This created our need to tie into some type of spiritual afterlife. Consequently religions of all types have evolved over the ages. And today as has been true throughout our history, religions zealots believe other religions are wrong to the point of killing to prove their point.

Why is it people can't see or understand the mysteries of our universe, but accept what scientists tell us about it? Why is it such a problem for people to acknowledge and accept the existence of a universal power? I'll refer to this entity as a universal power, universal energy, universal consciousness, or even a universal spirit.

Is there really a god of your choice, or no god?

How can I answer this any better than I can explain the mysteries of our universe? Am I saying you must believe in God? No and yes. No, meaning there may be other ways an expression of God manifests. Again history produces a god or gods for various religions. These gods throughout history come in many names. Even today, god or gods come in many forms and names. I believe mankind needs to believe!

Consequently yes, I do believe in a god as a spiritual power. Therefore, I believe all gods representing every theology are good and vital for sustenance and morality. They fulfill our need to provide for a civil society and our belief that our existence here is not all there is. Therefore I firmly believe all religions are uniquely tied into a universal power—or if you prefer, a universal consciousness. So one could logically assume that as we are part of this universal consciousness, then a god power manifests itself through each and every human being alive on Earth. Is there more proof of this power than of the way our universe was created or how it works? No. But I do know when tapping into this power, it works absolutely!

Furthermore, I believe this universal power is expressed and acknowledged at every level of our existence. Again I draw on the work of Deepak Chopra, whose *Seven Spiritual Laws of Success* informs us that a universal power (he refers to it as a Universal Mind) is not only responsible for coordinating the grandest gestures, such as the alignment of billions of galaxies, but also enables the subtlest perfections, such as the way in which our bodies consist of millions of specialized cells each of which exist solely to perform its singular function and which collectively operate the most complex and majestic of beings.

How can you open your mind to a spiritual or universal power?

Have you ever wondered why when going to bed at night bothered by a deep concern, you may suddenly awaken with a solution? How does this happen? Learned people have proven that humans have subconscious minds that are constantly active and working. However, these subconscious minds seem to work without our conscious knowledge. Writers have believed over many centuries that if our mind is tied to a subconscious mind, one we may not be aware of in our awake state, then chances are our subconscious mind is also tied into a universal consciousness.

As we proceed, I hope you will open up your mind to a belief I have. *It is my conviction that every human being on Earth is tied into a universal power, which may be called a universal spirit or universal consciousness.* This is why affirmations or prayers enter your subconscious where they are in turn instantly connected to a universal consciousness. Are you still with me? I believe they are connected! I do think some day scientists will be able to prove this connection, though perhaps not in my lifetime.

In fact there is a special method you can use to tap this unseen power. Whether you do or don't have religious beliefs, keep an open mind and I'll introduce or possibly reintroduce you to methods that work and bring exciting results. In chapter 13, I'll touch on some sound and simple ideas that may help you open doors to great good, prosperity, and happiness in your life!

How can using this power be a scary yet exciting proposition?

Let's first discuss the subconscious mind's interrelationship with a universal power and reasons this special power exists. In general terms, we've put forth propositions of how it exists and later why it can work for you. Most people use this power without realizing it. How often have you wished for something, then wished for it over and over again? Finally you set aside your wish and move ahead with your daily life, but then one day out of the blue, your wish is granted! Is this a coincidence? Have you ever requested a certain something to happen by wishing hard or through affirmations or prayers? In doing so you were affirming your deep-seated desires for something special to happen for you or someone close to you. You repeated your affirmations and prayers daily, then bingo, one day it happens: your desire, wish, or goal becomes reality. Why? Consider this thought: *"You will either be attracted to what it is you desire, or what you desire will be attracted to you."* I'm with those who believe there's a definite tie between a subconscious mind and a neutral, always awake universal consciousness that I prefer to call a universal power. When you use it for good and it works, it's both scary and exciting.

Why should you beware of right-wing religious thinkers?

Back in chapter 3 I wrote about my personal business failure as a means to illustrate how a person can make a comeback. I was in my mid-forties during this time. As I'd always been goal-oriented, I was constantly reviewing my goals and making current updates. But I needed more in my life. In my desire to reach out for something more, something giving me an extra dimension allowing me a positive reinforcement, I was able to get a key from a father at our local church. Even though I had pretty much moved away from traditional religion, my Catholic upbringing was brought to the fore. At seven each morning I'd silently enter the church, light a candle for my mother, and repeat special affirmations. This routine gave me the strength to start the day. As a year passed, I was still mired in a negative, downward-spiraling business whirlpool. It was important I continue and reach out for anything else that could strengthen a positive mental resolve.

Then it happened: I was asked to attend a fellowship meeting for a nondenominational Christian group. Put yourself in my shoes for a moment—I'm a person who believes in goals and affirmations and a positive mental attitude. I was invited to a gathering held in a conference room at a Mexican restaurant that serves beer and wine. As dinner was served, I noticed I was the only one who'd ordered a beer. At first I wasn't thinking too much about it, but it seemed all eyes were on me. Suddenly a speaker got up and began preaching the Bible's version of fire and brimstone. He then startled me by requesting, no *insisting*, that each person come up and accept Jesus Christ as his personal savior. The speaker looked directly at me. I was frozen in my seat. I felt beads of sweat popping from every pore, my whole body becoming wet with perspiration as my shirt became drenched. As diners made their way up to be saved, I found an opening and bailed out the side door. Why was I so affected?

First, let me say we must be kind to evangelists who fervently believe in their heart and soul that you must do exactly as they say if you want to be saved and don't want eternal damnation. However, as well-intentioned as these fervent believers are, be more than a little wary of their message. Think for yourself and stay strong in your own convictions. Likewise, beware of the zealot Muslims who say if you are an American unbeliever of their faith, you are the devil and must be destroyed—plus all their other "ifs" on why it *must* be their way or no way. Beware of extreme fundamentalism in any religious group. To me, the very definition of *fundamentalist* is someone who would betray his own religious teachings of love with hate and killing. Right-wing religious sects proliferate throughout our world by teaching children from infancy their ideas of right and wrong. That's fine as long as it doesn't take away people's fundamental rights of freedom and choice.

I believe advocating murder in order to eliminate nonbelievers is and has been the cause of most wars throughout history. When children are being indoctrinated as to their martyrdom and death of others as means to salvation and perpetuation of their "truth," mankind is in for a long haul in trying to open these young people's minds to freedom of thought and expression.

So, back to the beginning: why was I so affected by the fellowship meeting? Possibly because when our hearts and minds feel pressure from outside influences allowing no quarter, our internal self rebels against what it may not or cannot believe in. I'd like to think of God as a universal power that permeates all existing theologies and nonreligious thinking—a universal spirit that exists in every human being and essentially ties us all together.

As a means to open up our minds, let's explore more esoteric and possibly fathomless ideas. Okay, let's assume you can't get your thoughts around an idea of a universal power. Answer this: how can a tiny seed grow into a mighty oak or towering redwood?

How does a tiny acorn grow into a mighty oak?

How does a human grow from a microscopic seed?

Explain how a microscopic seed inside a female womb can become a full grown human being?

Why haven't the greatest minds figured out the beginning and end of our universe?

Our first ancestors must have felt Earth was their universe. In their minds, Earth was also flat. It apparently took thousands of years to dispel what man felt was a correct order of things: our sun rotated around the earth; we walked on a flat surface; this was man's center of the universe. However, man began to use science to come up with such heresies as our Earth was round, gravity held us on it, and apparently there was much more out there than man could see or understand. Of course many of these early scholars were either ridiculed or burned at the stake as heretics. Most men believed in what they could see, not outlandish theories of the newly known, unseen, and certainly not understood. Man continues his search into the universe and mysteries of how it began and how it may end.

Let's assume most people take for granted the Big Bang theory of the beginning of our universe. If so, explain this: what was there before the Big Bang'? So we're back to man can't see it, doesn't understand it, but accepts there being something out there with no beginning that has no end! It does create a short circuit in most people's minds to contemplate and attempt to understand the mystery of our universe. Man has a beginning and an end; animals have a beginning and an end; plants and all other living things have a beginning and an end—why not our universe? So, as man goes along accepting scientific theories on faith, it's no stretch to understand why all religions of the world are also accepted on faith alone. Although there currently exists no scientific understanding of a universal power, I'd like to have you give this notion the benefit of the doubt while you learn how it could positively impact your life.

Science and theology: How are they similar?

A definition of science is something like this: *The domain of knowledge by the systematic study of nature.* Theology means: *The rational and systematic study of religion and its influences, and of the nature of religious truth.* In a book I once read, a comment by U. S. Anderson caught my attention. Loosely stated, it went something like this: "At the end of the day when scientists climbed to the very top of the peak of knowledge, finally having uncovered all their questions regarding our universe, guess who was waiting at the top, giving them a helping hand upward? The theologians!"[10] Man needs both, but who's right? One might say it's the scientists; however, does science have all the answers? No! Does religion have all the answers? No! The unknown has created a need for religious faith. If man can't see it, can't feel or touch it, or can't come close to understanding it, faith takes over. A definition of faith: *"Belief in a supernatural power or powers that control human destiny, an institution expressing belief in divine power."* It appears both scientists and theologians are searching and expressing their own theories of life and our universe. It would also seem this search will be on going until the end of time!

Is it possible that man is or can be God?

Years ago, I was a member of an exercise gym. I met many interesting people on workout days. One gentleman in particular was a local teacher and good fellow. He also participated in a fundamental Christian church group as a lecturer, etc. Consequently, there would be inadvertent conversation that quite often led back to his idea of basic biblical truths. We had a small group of energetic business and salespeople meeting every couple of weeks to share books and ideas as a sort of mastermind motivational group. We all had similar ideas about some sort of universal power. One day when our Christian friend began quoting chapter and verse, I though it was time to hit him with my new theory. I told him I was God! I tried to explain, but he became apoplectic, got back into his street clothes, and disappeared.

Had he not been so shocked, I would have explained as follows: There is a universal power that can be interchangeable with what some might call a spiritual power. I believe this would have met with his agreement. Then I would have continued by explaining the following:

---

[10] *Andersen, Uell. Three Magic Words. No. Hollywood, CA: Wilshire Book, 1980.*

if there is a universal power or spirit that is in every human being on Earth, it ties us all together. If this energy comes through each and every one of us and we are all tied into it, then it would be a God power emanating from us. So I conclude I'm God. But I would quickly add, "So are you and everyone else on Earth. We are all tied into this God power and it comes out through each of us."

Do you think he would have bought it? This we do know for sure—we exist only due to unseen powers, powers we neither have any control over nor understand. It is amazing how learning to tune into this power can have such incredible results when setting goals, whether they are personal or business ones. I do believe there must be a universal power that comes through us and is part of all of us. And I know from firsthand experience that by using the goal-setting methods I've outlined in this and prior chapters, you will be guaranteed great success. Doing so will also reduce the intense pressures of running an active business enterprise. If this universal power or spirit is a God power, then it encompasses all religions and even people with no religious beliefs.

Chapter 13
Be Careful! You Become What You Think
—————————— $ ——————————

***How do we convert and tap all of the power given
us and create prosperity beyond our dreams?***

We need to be able to tap into our universal power. When I was a young man, I recall how my mother would pray with her rosaries over and over again to relieve a problem she may have had or to help someone in need. You see my mother had this unusual gift to be able to pray for others and obtain positive outcomes for them. As a younger man, I thought she may have had unusual powers. But years later I began to recognize people of all religious faiths as well as nonbelievers had similar powers. I believe through conscious concentration (which may be called prayers, meditation, or affirmations), a person can visualize a positive outcome to problem areas. Focusing on these affirmations twice a day can create results some might consider miraculous or magical.

As I mentioned earlier, stay with your affirmations; however, it's very possible that what you desire may come about quite differently than you hoped, yet indirectly fulfill your needs in a positive way. It's important to have a positive attitude toward how you interact with people and ideas and what you may wish for others. Many things contribute to your success, and I firmly believe the life energy you expend, whether positively or negatively, is returned to you in spades. So if we choose to spend our life energy in ways that bring joy and prosperity to others, we can be assured the same for ourselves.

Why does goal setting work?

When I was a boy, my family had a small dairy ranch. Fortunately I had two older brothers taking the brunt of the grunt work necessary to keep a dairy business going. For those of you unfamiliar with the duties involved, let me mention a few: up by 3:30 or 4:00 a.m. to round up dairy cows and bring them into a staging area for entrance into the barn stanchions. Milking cows by hand and by machine. Having excrement from cows' tails hitting our faces as we went through our milking process. Cleaning out very smelly and ugly barnyard gutters after milking. Hauling hay to our cow barns from our fields, usually in 100 degree temperature, plus much much more in "go-fer" chores.

As I grew into my early teens, I began to have a reoccurring thought: "Please when I grow up, let me do anything but work on a dairy ranch." In fact, in my late teens I kept repeating a transition-type goal: "If I could only graduate from milking cows to driving a truck picking up milk cans from dairies, I'd be the happiest guy in the world." So it happened, and from there I attended a local state university, driving a milk truck to get me through.

So, setting goals may be no more then planting ideas in you mind, correct? It may be as simple as that, but why does it work? You may have a wish deeply held, and you find yourself constantly thinking about it. Without our understanding how our conscious mind feeds our subconscious mind, our wish may still come true. (Although how this happens is still miraculous to me.) Over many years of reading authors of positive thinking-type books, I found a common thread running through their thoughts on goal setting. By organizing your desires into written goals and daily reviewing them, your conscious mind feeds your goal into your subconscious mind, which never sleeps, then your subconscious mind translates your goals into actions by placing you in a position to fulfill your deepest desires.

How can you be directed to your goal while those who can help achieve it are directed to you as well?

What is so incredible is how daily review of your goals can direct you to either people or things allowing you to achieve your goal. What's even more incredible is how people and things are directed to you. Your subconscious mind is always on duty; it's working for you whether you are awake or asleep. By having your conscious mind constantly reminding your subconscious of what it is you want, you have this extra power working for you 24/7. You may go for some time wanting to realize a certain goal in which you have invested much energy in affirming and thinking about it, but nothing happens. Then suddenly one day there it is: your goal visualization, preparedness, and opportunity meet. It's magical, a miracle maybe? Or are these the results of a positive outpouring of mental energy? Absolutely!

Is it possible that by setting goals, you create an energy field that attracts what you desire?

Theories abound as to what, how, and why setting goals and constantly reviewing them works. I do believe your subconscious mind is linked to a universal power also referred to as a universal mind. There are skeptics who believe you must see a thing for it to be real, but I hope I dispelled some of this doubt in chapter 12. Can you see electricity, microwaves, TV or radio waves? How about X-Rays, UVA rays, or any other types of unseen waves? No, we can't. However, although we can't see these energy waves, they can be detected, and although invisible, they can be perceived. Likewise, I feel there must be an energy field that is unknown and unseen but allows our subconscious mind to interact with an unseen universal mind. Some day science may reach a point where it may be able to perceive this special energy force just as it has other kinds of unseen waves.

How can laying out daily, weekly, monthly, and annual goals focus your attention?

I recall my first flirtation with goal setting. Remember, earlier I mentioned I was brought up on a dairy ranch, then later graduated to driving the milk trucks picking up ten-gallon cans of milk. This allowed me to continue my education. Then I became a young father of one, then two, then three, then four daughters in a six-year span. So in my twenties, I had up to three jobs at once to help keep our family fed, clothed and sheltered. This did not leave any time to plan, even if I knew what goal setting or planning was, because at this point, I was too busy reacting to life's basic needs.

Then at age twenty-nine it happened: I was given an opportunity to work as a life insurance salesman in my little county, and presto, a new world opened up to me. Once I had been trained and became a solid company insurance producer, my manager took a much greater interest in me. At year's end he gave me a piece of notepaper and advised me to write down every single goal my heart desired and wanted accomplished in the following year. It could be sales goals or personal goals. He also suggested I make them realistic, but not restrict myself. "Big enough to make you run!" he said (which meant to me goals that were higher then my expectations). He then continued, "I'm going to put this list of ten items you've laid out in an envelope and place it in my drawer. At the end of next year, I'll hand your envelope back to you."

I wrote out several goals I felt could not be achieved in a year. At the end of the year, was I ever surprised to read every goal I had written down had been accomplished, almost like a magician had waved a magic wand. Two of them were monumental. One was to be a Million Dollar Round Table member, something no one had accomplished it in my Northern California agency in twenty-five years. The other was to build a brand new custom home for my family. I did!

How did this miraculous thing happen, I asked myself? I then began reading a series of books regarding goal setting. I was thirty years old when I read the first book that truly made an impression on me, *Think and Grow Rich* by Napoleon Hill. He talked about goal setting and about giving more then full value, as well as thinking positive. I continued reading, starting with two books by U. S. Anderson, *Three Magic Words* and *The Magic in Your Mind*. These opened my eyes to the power of the subconscious mind and universal laws. Then after auditing a Dale Carnegie course, I read *The Power of Positive Thinking* by Norman Vincent Peale. In between I read many other books with the same common thread running through them all. Later I read

Winning Through Intimidation by Robert Ringer, an irreverent book on how to turn the tables on those trying to intimidate you. Finally the coup de grace was Deepak Chopra's *The Seven Spiritual Laws of Success* that I first read at age sixty. It has become my little living bible, as for me it encapsulated the teachings of most others in beautiful prose.

As I've already discussed, your subconscious mind needs to be fed information from your conscious mind. My experience has taught me that when you review your goals through affirmations twice daily, you are keeping these goals freshly imprinted into your subconscious mind. Let's call it giving your subconscious mind a sense of urgency. An intense desire tied into your daily review of goals helps stimulate your always-working subconscious. Your subconscious in turn directs your conscious mind to the very thing or things you desire most. Even though at first I had only looked at my goals once in a year and they still became real, I believe it was due to the incredible concern and burning desire I had to succeed, to make my family proud and to show naysayers I could do it! Since then reviewing my goals daily by affirmations has been a must.

Why do people spend more time planning annual vacations than annual goals?

Do you have acquaintances spending days and weeks planning an annual vacation trip? Have you experienced this yourself? Who hasn't, right? It's quite understandable to plan carefully for a big annual opportunity for your three *R*s—rest, recreation, and relaxation. It is very important and therapeutic to get away from work and worry and have bonding time with your family. Unfortunately, most people don't recognize that if they spent as much time planning their annual and lifetime goals as they do their annual vacations, they could greatly enhance their own standard of living. But hey, planning vacations is exciting while plodding along with annual goals may seem ho hum and boring. However, once people begin to understand the power of goal setting and this incredible new dimension offered them, they can then reorganize their efforts and make it part of their daily, weekly, monthly, and yearly essentials. And so can you!

Can expressing your personal goals to others keep them from being realized?

Have you ever confided to people close to you the specific goals or plans you were hoping to achieve only to have them throw cold water in your face? There are times you have to be very careful not to bare your soul to those around you. Why? Criticism creates doubts and robs you of your excitement and enthusiasm. Quite often other people will express their thoughts about your stated life goals in a negative way. There are times when laying out your goals for everyone to see may attract negative comments that may create doubts in your mind and a loss of personal enthusiasm. Remember: they're not in your shoes and haven't a clue as to your desires—they're merely creating doubts and fears that in turn undermine your positive thoughts and feelings. So be careful to whom you express your goals, as there are times you must keep these goals intimately yours, for example, when the goal is of an extremely personal nature or if it's regarding business plans where leaked information could derail you. However, there are times, especially in business goals, to let your associates in on what you are shooting for. It helps get them excited so they in turn can help you help them help you!

What's the best time to review your goals?

There are many theories as to when and how often you should read or mentally recite your goals. I believe your conscious mind feeds information into your subconscious mind, which in turn taps into a universal mind or power. Consequently the more often you repeat your affirmations daily, the greater opportunity there is for your subconscious to be interacting with your universal mind that generates solutions through your subconscious back to your active mind. It works!

One area that remains clear is this: if you want successful outcomes to goal setting, you *must* read or recite your goals in a timely manner. Some say you must recite or mentally review them first thing in the morning and before bedtime. I do believe twice a day is excellent, but if this is difficult, once a day is a must. As we've outlined above, "affirmations are magic."

How are affirmations and prayers similar?

Affirmations and prayers do overlap in their meanings. It's very possible some people not involved in organized religion may feel awkward if they mention they are praying versus affirming. Here's some definitions of each found in the Word Perfect thesaurus:

1) **"An affirmation is a statement asserting the existence or truth of something"**
2) **"The act of affirming or asserting something"**
3) **"A solemn declaration that serves the same purpose as an oath (if an oath is objectionable to the person on religious grounds),"** an **"avowal, an assertion"**

In comparison, prayer can be defined in these ways:

1) **"Worship"**
2) **"Reverent petition to a deity"**
3) **"Earnest or urgent request"**
4) **"A fixed text used in praying"**
5) **"Someone who prays to God"**

You can choose either word as a means of expressing your goals. I use *affirmations* as the preferable one as it may have a broader appeal and not conflict us by mixing religion with personal and business goal setting. Regardless, once your desires are expressed and repeated daily, miracles happen!

How do you determine what's most important in your life?

Most people march through life taking what comes with no specific plan. (This may come as a bit of a surprise, right?) These people take the line of least resistance, which may not be a bad thing, as they may never have ulcers. Then again, they may not focus on what they really want or is most important to them, consequently going through life wondering what could have been.

This does not have to happen to you! Let's assume there are several things you feel strongly about. You may even be passionate about them. It could be your relationship with a loved one such as your spouse, your girlfriend or boyfriend, or your special partner in life. It could be your children, your parents, or any and all of the above. It could be your biggest drive in life is to achieve personal and financial success. Or it could be that you want to create a fortune or at least a nest egg that allows your golden years to be free from financial pressures.

Is it possible to achieve all you fervently wish for? Sure, there are those who have lucked out in life by being in the right place at the right time. However, the odds of this happening to people is infinitesimal—it's like the luck of the draw in being born into wealth or hitting the lottery—just an exciting accident of fate. But for most of you, there needs to be a tried and true methodical approach to having a fair chance at getting what it is you most wish. First let's take a look at how you spend an average working day.

What do we do with our twenty-four hours per day?

It has been written and proved most people want some control over their lives, but seem to not be able to grasp or develop a method they can understand and use successfully. How often have we heard people say, "Boy, I've got to lose some weight," yet they haven't a clue how to develop a specific plan to make it happen? Or, if they do have a plan, they can't seem to carry it out. So you might say, "Well, according to this book, all you need is a goal and a desire and your subconscious does the rest, right?" Yes and no! Yes, a fervent desire can direct you to your goal, but no, not if you don't feed your subconscious on a daily basis. But there's more, much more. What you do each day and how you spend your time during every twenty-four hour period sets a pattern for what happens each day, then each week, then each month, then each year, then each lifetime.

Every day of your life is another precious one; you can benefit from it or you can waste it. It's imperative you develop an organized approach as to what you do every working day and how you spend your weekends. Help yourself by making a list of how you expect to spend each hour of your day. It's amazing how setting specific times for daily business meetings can keep you on your toes and motivated to get things done in a timely fashion.

However, you also need to give yourself some flexibility so as to maintain your sanity. One of the ways to get a handle on what you do each day is using your appointment book or calendar. If you don't have an appointment book, get one. Computer literate people are using modern programs designed to give you the latest in hi-tech appointment planning. Studying your appointment book or diary gives you a clear idea of your work patterns and how they tie into your family time, recreation time, physical fitness time, and time for self-development. Please refer back to chapter 2, "Rethinking and Retooling for Success" and the seven safe harbors of life.

Can anyone stay focused without goals?

We all know people with a burning desire so great nothing will get in their way to achieving a specific goal. These people may not have written goals, but their internal desire to achieve outweighs anything else in their lives. One might call what they have an obsession. Regardless, an obsession is an energy force that can ultimately propel us to accomplish our goals. Most people need to have an organized way to set and review goals so they can move toward accomplishing them. Can you imagine taking a vacation trip across the United States and back without a specific road map with places to visit, places to stay, and time spent along the way? It's possible you could, but you might end up like the people in the movie *Lost in America*.

Goals help you zero in on what's most important to you now! As you succeed in accomplishing prior goals, you need to be constantly reviewing your needs and desires to formulate updated ones. Your reaching one goal usually sets the stage for reaching another, then another. This is good. Remember, you must review your goals on a daily basis for best results. Daily affirmations keep your pipeline to your subconscious mind on full alert. All you then need to do is continue your normal duties and activities and let your subconscious carry the rest of the load for you. It works!

How must you vary and reshape goals if they don't appear to be what you wanted and needed?

Quite often you may not realize your goal has been reached. Our subconscious may direct you to your goal on an indirect path. You may be surprised to reach a goal in an unexpected way, and at first react negatively to it, not realizing a greater power is leading you. At other times you may think your goal is simply too great or too hard to reach. But don't give up. Remember, "the light at the end of the tunnel" may not be there now, but it's possible if you take a left turn from your current tunnel into a new one, then make a right turn, eureka, there's the light. If all else seems to fail, you may have to pursue your goal by pushing in a new direction. *Do not* force a goal and become a "Bloody Pulp"; a right path will open up to you and beckon you to its achievement with effortless ease.

Do you become what you think?

Whether you are obsessed with an incredible desire and think about it constantly or you daily review goals, either way you do become what you think and do! The act of constantly feeding your conscious thoughts into your subconscious causes a chain reaction that in turn becomes a reality in your life. So beware—once you have placed your desires into this energy field called your subconscious mind that in turn is sucked into a vortex called your universal mind, a potent universal power takes hold that can lead you to your promised land. It goes without saying you wish for the good things in life and positive things for you and your family. Good creates an aura that permeates everything you do and touch, and this goodwill sparks a positive energy that propels you to your most desired things in life. You do become what you think—and life is good!

Chapter 14
How to Do Less and Accomplish More

—————————— $ ——————————

I F YOU ARE A devotee of Deepak Chopra, as I seem to be, then
you may recognize my question in the above chapter heading. It's
possible you have an incredible zeal and enthusiasm for accomplishing
whatever is set out before you. This is good, but it can also cause you
to become wound up tightly. Whenever you have this unrelenting
pressure to succeed, it may affect your ability to focus, and it could
affect your ability to function. It may even cause you to break down
physically as well as mentally. That's why I love using this mixed
metaphor: "Involved Detachment." It may seem to be a contradiction
in terms, but it can be your lifesaver as you're confronted daily with
your struggle to move ahead. You have this driving desire and need to
accomplish a certain something, but remember: keep your burning
desire alive, but back off from the results.

Why should you step back from a situation and allow it to happen?

Earlier in the book, I asked you to consider if in the past you
might have pursued a special goal with the zeal of a crusader. You had
to achieve it on your own terms and in no other way. You insisted it
had to be exactly as initially written out. You felt it must be your way

or no way! Quite often you may believe your success has to be exactly how you've defined your goal. However, this is not true, so don't jam it! Things change, circumstances change, and your subconscious mind that is plugged into your universal consciousness knows much more than you do. Give achieving your goal a good shot, but then back off and let it happen.

What negative forces are at work when a situation is forced?

In a prior chapter, I articulated how forcing situations may cause you to become a "Bloody Pulp." I recall a goal I had in my earlier days. I purchased thirty acres next to a major freeway including a closed former Shell Oil service station. One of my mastermind motivational group associates was a building designer. We developed a plan for mixed use development on this site. We'd have commercial property along our freeway off-ramp, plus an attractive retail buffer strip serving the needs of a housing tract, which would be a planned unit development with duplexes, detached and attached homes, and even manufactured housing. Boy was I hot to get this done. To obtain all of our entitlements (which included all of our engineering for sewers, electricity, roads, curbs, and gutters plus carrying costs and taxes on our land purchase), our cost approached six figures.

You have all heard of timing, haven't you? There's the adage, "Timing isn't everything—it's the only thing." However, I failed to take heed. The hot market of the 1970s was cooling off. I was advised to back off, but "no," I shouted to any listener, "I cannot and will not stop my mission to get this project started. To not do so would be a big negative. I'm not a quitter!" By January 1980 our nation's interest rates went sky high, and our bank offered to finance our deal at 16.5%. Nothing penciled out: my projects turned into losing propositions, and double digit interest rates continued for three years, a historical record for our country. Due to my single-minded efforts to make it work irrespective of the consequences, all my work and financial investment was lost, and I became a "Bloody Pulp"—end of story!

There are telltale signs you should pick up on when trying to make something happen. When you start to feel resistance, it's not necessary to stop cold and run off, but you need to have an ear to the ground. Resistance needs to be understood by trying to understand its root causes. The lyrics of Kenny Rodger's song "The Gambler" that you need to "Know when to hold 'em and know when to fold 'em"[11] are absolutely right on.

What happens when our ego causes us to control situations?

How often have you encountered a situation where your need for one-upmanship, "keeping up with the Joneses," or making it happen your way has led you into tragic results? Inevitably, the cause is your *ego*, my friends! You feel your powerful thinking can overcome all. Consequently you begin to control people around you, and actually you begin to unknowingly manipulate them. Why? Because you feel you are 100% right—you want this to happen, and you know better then anyone what's right for you and what's right for them. By then you feel that by controlling your own situation, you will make it happen your way. But at what cost does this happen? It's very difficult to control our ego needs. However, success is achieved when all the pieces flow together and you struggle mightily to let your selfless self emerge while letting the chips fall where they may. Result: you may have a chance to achieve a harmonious solution to your desires.

Why is seeking control over people a waste of time and energy?

We have all heard the saying, "Earn people's respect." Can this be done if your associates feel they're being bowled over by your blind ambition to do it your way? So how do you balance your intense inner need to do it your way and still earn respect and appreciation from your associates?

There are many factors entering into this equation. You must be able to have a give-and-take with those surrounding you. They too must have a feel for what it is you're trying to accomplish. Allowing them to share in some way is always a winner; move forward, but listen closely so you can hear what they are saying and adjust your game plan accordingly. Remember, resistance creates negativism, and if you have to constantly fight it, **you're using up negative unproductive energy**. Rather than seeking power and controlling everyone around

---

[11] *Kenny Rogers, "The Gambler," Don Schlitz, The Gambler Soundtrack, United Artists LP 934, 1978.*

you, allow for feedback to get you on the right track. This allows you to keep from wasting time and energy while simultaneously gaining the added respect of your associates.

Can you create true happiness by focusing on money acquisition alone?

Have you ever met someone who seems to have achieved a high degree of financial success (in other words, they're loaded), yet they don't seem to be happy? They feel they must create even more wealth to find true happiness. But it never happens as they're never satisfied. **It would seem true happiness comes when** money flows from success, **rather then money being the one and only pursuit in someone's life**! To be truly successful, you need to fit together many elements to bring a special balance in your life. You must follow the essentials such as how you live each day; how you handle your diet, exercise, and rest periods; and how you relate to your children, your business associates and especially your spouse or special person in your life. Yes, of course money is important, but money alone does not buy you happiness—it's whether you achieve a balance in your life that eventually gives you true happiness and prosperity.

Through all of this you must consistently attend to your physical and recreational needs so they can give back to you good health and peace of mind. There's nothing wrong about focusing on wealth as part of your security, but keep it in balance. Real wealth comes from not just creating it, but from how you maintain a balanced life that provides you love, which in turn gives you tranquility and a sense of real accomplishment. This then is true success!

Can you step back and allow indirect results to work for you?

This has been a constant theme throughout this book. You may be getting tired of reading about it; however, your ability to deal with this concept may be your key to a prosperous, well-balanced, and positive business and personal life. You must always levy a forceful attack on whatever you choose to go after as this is essential. And yes, you must have unwavering zeal in trying to reach your goals. However, you may reach a point, let's call it a critical mass, where you find one stumbling block after another in your final path to achievement. In your attempts at smashing through, you may be on the verge of becoming that lifeless body on the other side of the wall. At this point, you must allow an outside power, let's call it your universal consciousness, to help you determine your correct path. It's tough to consider options when you have geared up with only one thought in mind of achieving your desired and specific goal. However, don't become that "Bloody Pulp" as you must bite the bullet and redirect your strategy.

How can taking the line of least effort be the best way?

Let's assume you had a goal, but you find your prize slipping away. The harder you try, the worse things become. The pressure on you becomes unbearable, and you are ready to toss in the towel. But don't despair and don't give up. Instead step back and allow your situation to evolve. Your goal is out there to be reached, so merely redirect and go with the flow. This may be called "doing less and accomplishing more." It's important to have an out when your pressure point becomes unbearable. By stepping back, you take the immediate heat off of yourself, which then opens up a field of unlimited possibilities. Now that the heat has been removed, you can think in a more objective manner. Nevertheless, don't take your eyes off the results as a path to achieving your goal will become clear. It may not have been what you first thought, but in most cases it ends up being your best course of action.

Why does fear of failing cause us to push harder?

Insecurity can both work for you and against you. Most people have some sort of insecurity; it can be your looks, your height, your weight, your lack of education, your dysfunctional family, or just your not having the financial resources to get things in life you've always wanted. Insecurity is a feeling riding just below your subconscious thinking. Insecurity can be a driving force for good or a driving force for evil. Let's work on how it can produce evil in your life. Negative feelings about your self-worth can cause almost every imaginable negative to happen. When this occurs, your overall attitude regarding your belief systems such as your accomplishing set goals, your relationship with your spouse and family, and your relationships with past and present associates begins to erode and you may find yourself in a state of depression. These behaviors are easily triggered when you are trying desperately to achieve but all fails, as that's when a failure syndrome may take over. You reach a point where you feel you don't deserve to achieve, and consequently you are forever relegated to failure.

On the other hand, fear of failure can be an incredible force for good. If you're fortunate enough to have the inner determination to show the world you are as good as anyone and better then most, then you can use your phenomenal inner drive to fight on to some sort of victory. Even if your worst fears materialize and you do fail, guess what? Your desire is so great, your need to prove yourself so powerful, you jump right back in and fight again. This time you evaluate what and where you went wrong, determine a new plan of action, **learn from prior mistakes**, and go for it. Just don't lead with your chin— remember the "Bloody Pulp."

Why is it important to let those around you live up to their potential?

As you move along with your new enterprise or an old one with new ideas and a new plan of action, your greatest opportunity for success depends on your key people. Most often a start-up operation is a one or two-person enterprise; however, as your small company begins to grow, you will need to add some good people to help perpetuate a successful operation. As you add a person here and there, your growth continues to create new needs that must be filled by your newly hired associates. If you have good, hardworking associates evolving into an area of company growth where they may be the perfect fit, give 'em a shot!

This is where you need to be flexible with an associate's ability to handle increased responsibility in new, growing areas of your company. An example may be where an associate may have a problem in dealing with the sales operation side of your company, but may have excellent skills in dealing with all your hi-tech needs (i.e., installing, troubleshooting, and keeping your firm on the hi-tech cutting edge). Quite often when a shift of responsibility occurs with a particular associate and your associate shows a grasp of his/her new job duties, the result may be a resounding business success.

What do you think this exciting success and growth for your company means to your associate? Personal growth in both income and job satisfaction! Bringing out that special something you recognize in your associate's talent can catapult that person into helping create and putting the building blocks together for an exciting, growing, and dynamic company. By watching for latent talent and abilities in your good people with good attitudes, you will increase their pride a thousand fold, which in turn results in an exciting synergy that can help create the wealth you can all share!

How can you take the line of least resistance and redirect associates to their areas of strength?

As your small enterprise starts to take shape and begins to create income that can only be sustained by adding new, good people, a metamorphosis takes shape. You need sharp people with an aptitude for management. How do you get these people? Two ways: go out into the work marketplace and pay top dollar for someone having the perfect credentials, or elevate an associate in your current operation.

Giving an opportunity to someone within your current organization may have a drawback or two. What happens if you give a current associate a chance and the person blows it? How do you keep a good person who is doing great work otherwise but incapable of fulfilling a new role? You don't. However, I firmly believe your best strategy is allowing someone within your growing company to step up. Why? Because that person has a feel for how your company ticks. and after a period of time you should have a feel for your person's talent potential. You can put one of your associates into a key position based on your knowledge of that person's strengths.

However, when you give people an opportunity to step up, they may be reluctant or unsure of their abilities to meet your standards. Encourage them by reminding them this is an experiment so they should give it a chance. By calling it an experiment, you have a better chance of retaining a valuable associate who may not cut the mustard.

However, nine times out of ten your gut-level feeling about your associate and your gentle nudge gives your associate a newly found confidence. Now all you have to do is step back and watch 'em grow!

How do you negotiate to recruit new blood?

Negotiations are the name of the game, but so is the attitude you sense during them. Finding a middle ground is a key element that comes into play in any kind of negotiation whether it's recruiting a new sales force associate or potential key management person or any type of business dealings. My experience lies more in the give-and-go we need to deal with when trying to recruit someone into our company's sales force as an independent contractor. First we push hard by detailing all our company's benefits, hitting hard on all of our company's strengths in terms of commissions, branch office opportunities, and regional management opportunities, as well as offering more then enough lender products they may broker through our company's sources.

As we are pushing our exciting benefits to this potential new independent contractor, we pause and watch for reactions. Generally there is a give-and-take as we answer questions they may have. We also listen to all the great offers they've had from the world's greatest companies. We counter this by showing how our smaller but dynamic company has greater upside in income, tremendous corporate support, etc. They may come back with a "yes, but" on every positive point we make. As both sides reach a point of potential agreement, our prospect may throw us a curve by demanding a much greater commission income plus guaranteed leads. In cases where a person seems to have a one-upmanship on everything we've presented by telling us how Company X can do more of all these things for them, our people are tempted to ask in jest, "Please give me the name of that company, I want to work for them myself!" As we discussed earlier in chapter 9, it's imperative both parties have a comfortable feeling so a final contract can be completed successfully. At some point we need to understand both parties must come to a center point or middle ground.

Why does chasing after someone cause more grief in the long haul?

How often have you tried to work something out with people—family, friend, business associate or client—and they drive such a hard bargain on their end of the deal that you finally succumb to their demands. But as the deals are implemented, all your nagging feelings about caving in come back to drive you nuts. You are stuck with something in which your anxious desire to get something caused you to give up much more then you should have. So it is with your negotiations to attract a new person to your firm. I've already mentioned catchwords such as *center point* and *middle ground*; let me now add *a point of equilibrium*. What do these catchphrases mean?

It all leads to how we must respond at a critical point in our negotiations. What we should do has been illustrated earlier (see chapter 9). You are making more concessions than your gut tells you is right, concessions you will regret that will come back to haunt you later. A positive solution and completion to your negotiations is when your interviewee and you reach a center point where each of you is nose to nose at the middle ground, our point of equilibrium, as then generally you'll have a deal that has an excellent chance of working. Beware: negotiating is one area where you can give too much and get too little.

Why does forcing solutions to problems merely create more problems?

Let's continue our example above regarding negotiating for key or top sales people. I outlined how jamming a deal together can occur because we feel it's a solution to our company's growth problem. Forcing solutions can also apply to any of your other business dealings, whether it be recruiting, developing marketing relationships, leasing office space, purchasing property, or any other area of decision making. Anytime you force a solution because it is expedient or because you want whatever it is in the worst way, you may solve an immediate problem, but open the door to new and possibly greater problems that will drain energy you could have been using in a positive way to further your company's success. On a personal note, this also applies to your decision making with your spouse and family, but whoa—that's a story for another time!

Your best approach in reaching a decision regarding any type of negotiations is to give it all you got. Go after whatever it is you want with the zeal of a warrior. Apply as much pressure as you can to reach an agreement, but when you feel you are reaching over the imaginary line, your point of equilibrium, then back off. I mean back off! Then let it come to you, see if the deal can still reach the center point and become workable for you. If it doesn't come together in what you feel is a fair an equitable way, walk away from it!

If it's a deal you're pushing and it's your negotiating party who wants to step back, try using the tried and proven method we've called an experiment. In this way both parties know it's a trial situation and if your deal doesn't work, you scrap it and walk away without anyone getting stuck. If it does work, hey fantastic—all parties are delighted and you can build from there.

Does all of this mean you must back off on your goals?

Absolutely not! Project your goals; continue the daily affirmations of your cherished objectives. Keep your idea of achieving your goals with the exciting results you expect. Just don't grab on so tight that you break instead of bend. If your goals don't quite turn out as you expected, redirect! Remember: don't change your goals, just your attachment to the results.

Chapter 15

Prosperity

───────────── $ ─────────────

OUR DISCUSSION ABOUT DEVELOPING habits reminds me of being fourteen and living on a small dairy farm in Northern California. My mother was essentially raising a family of three boys and two girls as a single mom. I was the middle child, with my two older brothers being old enough to have outside jobs to help support the family and keep the little dairy ranch afloat. My two younger sisters were only one and seven years old, so guess what? Yours truly got the unenviable job of milking the thirteen cows and cleaning out the barn morning and night, all the time attending school.

Every other week our little dairy ranch had its turn at receiving irrigation water from a main canal system. I'd divert water from the main canal to a smaller tributary canal that ended at our ranch. Then I'd divert the water between levies to keep our cow pasture growing. So who got the job of waking up at 1:30 a.m. and 4:30 a.m. to check and change the water gates? You guessed it. On irrigation nights, my mother's biggest job was to try and awaken a deep-sleeping young teenager. First she would pleasantly call out "George," which came out "Geoorrge" in Portuguese. Her next attempts were a louder and more demanding, "*Geoorrge*"! Once these initial attempts failed, the

"Mother of All Wake-Up Calls" took place. She would spit on her index finger, then run it across my eyelids! Yikes! I would fly out of bed and head for the bathroom yelling "dirty pool." But it worked every time. I'd slip on my black, heavy rubberized boots and plod out into the dark and damp night, hating every step. There's no question your upbringing is an essential force in creating a work ethic.

What does all this have to do with anything, you say? It's about *making your habits.* As my discussion draws to a close, I want to leave you with an important thought—while I have spent most of this book suggesting new habits, it's crucial that you learn how to integrate these habits into your daily life. I've searched for the reasons some people have a feel for developing positive habits and why others allow negative habits to take hold and drag them into a desperate lifestyle. It seems to me it is a combination of our built-in DNA and what we learn from our upbringing. It's a tough call to make as we all know siblings from a given family who have been brought up the same way, some surfacing to great success while others can't seem to get it going.

Somehow DNA, our gene pool, has to have a significant affect on who we become. We are all creatures of habit—the question is, did those habits come automatically due to our gene pool mix, or can childhood and adolescent experiences become stamped onto our subconscious creating a pattern for future positive responses? I'd like to think that regardless of our DNA, we can learn from negative experiences and develop positive habits that place us on a new course to a fulfilling life. So I'd like to tweak an old expression that goes, "In the beginning you make your habits, but in the end your habits make you" into something like this: *"In the beginning you may be taught good habits. If you stick to them, in the end these habits will make you!"* However, if you weren't taught good habits, a burning desire to change and learn and put to work new positive habits will take you as far as you have ever wished to go—and beyond.

Why is goal setting essential to your success?

As my twenty-ninth birthday was quickly arriving, I had become paranoid about turning thirty without a specific career opportunity opening up. My jobs were all dead-enders: no health benefits, no retirement benefits, and no opportunity for advancement. Having several jobs at once was imperative for me to earn enough to pay the house mortgage and feed a family consisting of me, a spouse, and four little girls. I was fearful of leaving my small town for possible but not assured opportunities in a larger city. Up to this age, I had gotten my creative juices flowing by playing and managing softball teams and town basketball teams while also managing a nonprofit weight training gym. I got my strokes from participating in all of these activities, but guess what? They provided no money and no future. I knew nothing of setting goals, let alone how to plan the activities needed to reach one.

During my twenties, I had been approached a number of times about entering the life insurance business as a sales representative in my little county. My answer was always, "Not interested." Why? My idea of a life insurance salesperson was guys walking up to a door, knocking on it, having the door open, introducing themselves, then having the door slammed in their faces. Sorry, not interested in pursuing a sales opportunity—no way, no how!

As each year in my twenties began ticking off and age twenty-nine was fast approaching, so were my work options **dwindling**. Finally I conceded to being interviewed for a life insurance position in my county. I started my training right after my twenty-ninth birthday. Scared to death, I nervously plunged into the insurance sales business. Surprise after surprise awaited me. It turned my life around both financially and mentally. Why? The life insurance company provided workshops, homework courses, regional office training, and seminars in financial planning. I was told I now was an independent contractor, my own boss; consequently I lived or died by my ability to make sales. In turn this taught me a sense of urgency on how to follow up and follow through and close that sale. It taught me how to set goals and how goal setting did work! As my income grew, I began to recognize a whole new world of opportunities lay ahead for me

I discovered goal setting is one of our most essential habits providing us a means to open a new door, step through it, and if successful, open another door, then another and another. As your small steps have a modicum of success, new and exciting opportunities open up to you so you can fly as high and as wide as your motivation, perseverance, and enthusiasm will allow. A great new world beckons, and the world becomes your oyster! In chapter 13, "Be Careful! You Become What You Think," I covered how you can use goal setting to your ultimate advantage. As I have outlined earlier, most people spend more time planning their annual vacation than their business, career, or family relationships. Goals (plans) need to be prepared the first of each new year, reviewed each day, updated each month, and fine-tuned each quarter. It's also important to project your goals over a five-year as well as a ten-year period. Do it—it works!

How can goal setting direct people and things to you (or you to them) to accomplish your desired goals?

I discovered the well-known secrets of goal setting in my own life. Here's one of the areas I first noticed it working for me. I'd set a specific goal, I understood that I must work very hard to scratch, claw, struggle, and fight to achieve it. I understood I must do it, only me, as no one would help if I didn't do it all on my own. I also believed I must take a direct path to achieving it. Wrong!

What I did discover was this: when you have written down a goal and you review it constantly, it's in the forefront of your conscious mind. It's then picked up by your subconscious mind. A magical thing begins to happen: you not only are led to people and things that allow you to accomplish your goal, but surprisingly people and things unexpectedly come directly to you to help you. Why? Because your subconscious mind is always working. This is why you need to be prepared for the possibility your goals may not be achieved as you first envisioned them, but rather indirectly. Your subconscious knows the best way. I don't know why for sure, but it works—try it!

Napoleon Hill, author of *Think and Grow Rich*, said it perfectly: *"What you conceive and believe you can achieve!"*[12] But how can that happen? Let's take your thinking, your desires, your goals to a level beyond your subconscious mind. The next step is where your subconscious is in tune and merged into a universal consciousness

---

[12] *Napoleon Hill. Think and Grow Rich, rev ed. (1937; repr., San Diego: Aventine Press, 2004).*

also referred to as a universal power or universal energy. There is a mystical or spiritual quality to this belief. I believe it is real and it works. A glimpse into this thinking is a song that touched me years ago, with lyrics by R. Kelly: **"I Believe I Can Fly"**:

> *If I can see it, then I can do it!*
> *If I just believe it, there's nothing to it*

By learning and working on keeping our ego in check as well as backing off from needing to control everyone and everything in our life, we can reach a point where our true, good, and honest self can emerge. Finding our true selves is not easy. It requires us to examine all we do. Every time we try to force issues, we in turn create resistance that applies pressure and affects our mental state. We need to avoid attachment to specific things, especially money. Quite often it's our deep insecurity that forces us into a "must have it or else" attitude that suggests a poverty conscience. Our true self must help our ego detach itself from specifics it feels it must have, such as the "keeping up with Joneses" syndrome.

Once we can detach ourselves from what our ego expects of us and deal with a life of give-and-go, a great pressure is released. You can back off by avoiding all the extreme temptations of having it all or forcing yourself to try to have it all. When you reach this stage in your life, you are now dealing with your true self, which in turn will attract to you wealth, health, and happiness.

You embody the qualities you envision, right?

Not only is it logical to assume what you think is who you become, but there is a preponderance of evidence staring us right in the face. Look in your mirror and check yourself out. Notice how your hair is combed, the type of clothes and shoes you wear, plus jewelry, watches, and so forth. Are your clothes crisp and pressed? How do you smell to others? What types of fragrances do you use, etc.? I'm not kidding. Almost every attribute someone notices about you is a product of your attention (or lack thereof) to personal details. When your conscious thinking is in slumber, automatically your subconscious mind continues to work. Thoughts have incredible power. *As you think, as you act, as you speak, as you look, so you are!*

Does diet and exercise matter?

I feel badly for people reaching middle age and beyond who are told by their doctors, "You must get exercise and eat right if you expect to live a normal life**span**." Let's take exercise, as most people who have not been involved in an organized exercise plan of any kind, taken physical education classes in school, played some form of sports, worked out in a health gym, hiked regularly, or done yoga, calisthenics, etc, have an extremely tough time learning how to develop a routine later in life and sticking with it. It's imperative to work in an organized time for some sort of daily exercise plan (it doesn't have to be a heavy duty program). It's best to work into it gradually and make it a lifetime habit—it works!

Eating: now there's a topic! It is beyond speculation that your eating and drinking habits make you who you are over the long haul. People think exercise alone can help you with working toward a desired weight, but no—your weight is affected by anything and everything you put into your mouth and swallow. It is 80% of what affects your weight, with the other 20% being exercise. However, exercise provides you with 90% of what it takes to feel good about yourself. Exercise provides both muscle toning and cardiovascular benefits. Keeping your body in shape keeps you sharp mentally. If you look good and feel good, it affects your relationships in business and on a personal level. You set an example for others and they enjoy being around you (unless of course you preach about it too much, as I'm doing here). Remember, keeping sharp, looking decent, and feeling good goes hand and hand with success! So, as you eat and as you exercise, so you are!

Is an entrepreneurial pursuit necessary for success?

Most working people live in a world where absolute financial security is everything. That's fine! However, for those of you itching to do something on your own, it may be worth it to take a plunge (see chapter 1). We live in the richest country in the world. Our United States has become a powerful, modern nation rivaling the great achievements of Egypt, Greece, and Rome. And guess what: we are here in the midst of this mighty country offering all these exciting opportunities for personal and business growth. If you are one of those undecided, but chomping at the bit to be an entrepreneur, you have to give it a shot. Remember: nothing ventured nothing gained. Besides trying and trying again is the American Way!

Our incredible country will continue to have great success as long as it continues to allow hardworking citizens (and yes, immigrants) the opportunity to start their own small businesses. In fact, quite often it's the people new to the United States who seem to see opportunities when others brought up here fail do so. It's possible a combination of blood, sweat, and tears and having the guts to find a way into a new and foreign environment gives immigrants the edge. Why? They have established themselves as risk takers by just showing up, and their glass is always half full! They are prepared to take on any challenge, any risk, any opportunity with the conviction they will succeed. You as established citizens of this fantastic nation have the same potential for unlimited achievement. You can fly as high and far and wide as you can possibly envision! Our mighty country will continue to be the flagship leading the world as long as it allows the economic blood and vitality brought on by anyone desiring the rewards of starting their own business. Most will succeed, and our United States is the stronger for it. This I believe!

Is the 'DY' Formula important in entrepreneuring?

Once you get into a start-up business opportunity, you do it all: create the business plan, order the merchandise, handle the bookkeeping, put together direct advertising, provide PR to your customers, set up networking to bring in buyers, make calls to sell and push your product—plus clean up each night. As you begin to have some success, you begin to recognize that *you* know best what to do in every facet of your fledgling enterprise.

But how do you build on this? You, on your own can do only so much, so you need to implement the DY Formula: Duplicate Yourself (review chapter 4 for the nuts and bolts of this formula). By having the ability to manage people and recruit and keep good ones, you can duplicate your own efforts many times over. This DY Formula allows you to create wealth with ease. Actually you can be doing less and accomplishing much more. As your new associates recognize your methods do work, you'll be developing a bond with them. This bond stems from sharing the knowledge and wealth with each associate you bring aboard, as from their success, your success becomes inevitable!!

Why be wary of the "Bloody Pulp" Theory?

It has been believed for decades that only by being aggressive, never taking no for an answer, and applying a religious zeal can you break through. You can accomplish any goal you wish to achieve. There is truth in this tied to the PMA or "Positive Mental Attitude" theory preached for many years. However, I have learned a little caution may be in order. Have you pursued a goal you were determined to accomplish? You'd been told, "you will encounter obstacles, so picture a mighty wall between you and your desire." Then according to the old PMA theories, here's what you must do: "If you can't go through it, go around it; if you can't go around, go over it; if you can't go over it, go under it; if none of these work, break through it!"

What happened to you when you tried breaking through it? I can answer that one. When every possible tactic has been used without success and you need to force the issue and break through the mighty obstacle, guess what? You become a "Bloody Pulp" (see chapter 9 for more details on this theory). So what do you do? You can't go over, under, around, or through it, so do you give up? No! You may have to keep going left or going right or make a 180-degree turn and try an opposite direction. By backing off and redirecting your energy in a new modified strategy, you may find a better albeit indirect path to accomplish what you had hoped. It may even be better than you originally conceived. Remember: smashing your way through to force a solution to achieving your goal gives you a "Bloody Pulp" as your result. Don't give up, don't quit, just take a different run at it—it works!

Can your associate relationships make or break you?

There's an old saying, "You can choose your friends, but you can't choose your relatives." Another old saying is, "Working partnerships are like a marriage." As we can choose a friend or in this case a working associate, it is a marriage, and like any marriage, you can either grow together or grow apart. You can never be sure that someone you bring aboard will grow and succeed as a partner associate. An additional old saying is, "Water seeks its own level." If you're fortunate enough to attract an associate who is a true like thinker, you can grow to a new level. Quite often new associates will talk the talk (agree with everything you lay out), but they can't walk the walk (i.e., they begin to stray from your company philosophy). At this point, it's best to separate sooner rather than later. As you know, "A bad apple spoils the barrel." Conversely, a positive, motivated associate not only grows with you, but creates a step up in your success!

Is there magic in sharing?

The Law of Giving: Way before reading Deepak Chopra's "laws of success," my company's corporate philosophy was: *"What you share will multiply and what you withhold will diminish."* There is a special magic in sharing. It applies to every facet of our lives. (Review chapter 11, "The Magic Power of Sharing.") It has a direct impact when you apply it to your business life just at it does in your personal life—no difference. People gravitate to those offering opportunities to create wealth. When you can offer new associates a direct sharing in wealth they've helped create, both you and your associates create a combustible element that can cause an explosion of profit growth for your enterprise. Sharing the wealth with good, highly motivated associates can take you as far and wide and high as your imagination, enthusiasm, and motivation allows!

Although I believe there's no question we are ultimately shaped by our habits, I'm hopeful this book points to a multitude of factors that can help you direct those habits. Prosperity comes in many forms. You must stir together a healthy, tasty stew of many factors that when properly combined lead to a fulfilling life's journey. An important part of the recipe of success is to not to lose sight of the universal power.

Here's a question I sense you might still be asking: "Is there a universal power?" I can only add I do believe our subconscious mind taps into one. I also believe someday scientists will be able to explain and theologians will accept that this power does exist. This discovery will turn scientific theory and religious teaching on its head. However, a merging of the two, as has been the case over our known history, will advance our ability to take advantage of this power rather than just pooh-poohing it. Sharing attracts the wealth of the universe—create wealth in others, and wealth, health, and prosperity will stream your way!

The opportunities for you and me to become a successful entrepreneur are one of the hallmarks of our great country of America. If followed, the tips provided in this humble book can provide you with rock-solid ideas on keeping and building your own business. Take what works for you and what may enhance your growth. And remember your only competition is the person you see in the mirror: it's the real you!

The End

(My thanks to Arturo Balderrama of Sacramento, California, for his six illustrations!)

"Back-to-back we can take on the world!"
George J. & Lana J. Trovao

*Picture taken in February, 2000 to
Commemorate our vow made in 1982.*

Born December 5, 1935, in Gustine, California, to Jose Martins Trovao and Diolinda Machado Castro Trovao.

My parents were born in Terceira, Azores, part of a nine-island chain belonging to Portugal. The islands lie in the Atlantic Ocean seven hundred miles or so due west of mainland Portugal. My parents came to America in the early 1900s because America was where money practically grew on trees! They were in for a big surprise. But hard work on a dairy ranch allowed them to raise five children and provide them with a taste of the terrific opportunities in this great and wonderful land of *America*. I'm grateful to them!

In this book I've tried to provide you a life-long history of my ups and downs and how you can gain from my insights within. I've enjoyed revealing some powerful truths about life, love, and work as well as our life journey. I want you as an entrepreneur to succeed. Your "Magic Wand" lies inside this cover!

George J. Trovao